When We Must Say Farewell

By

Karl E. Jennings

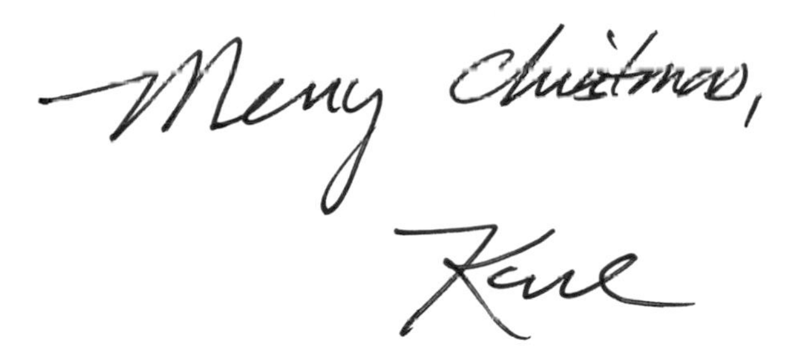

MARSHALL MICHIGAN
800PUBLISHING.COM

When We Must Say Farewell

Cover design by 2 Moon Press
307 W. Michigan Ave. Marshall Michigan 49068
800publishing.com

Author photo by Courtesy of Author

ISBN-13: 978-1-935805-85-4

First published in 2010

10 9 8 7 6 5 4 3 2

Published by 2 MOON PRESS
307 W. Michigan Ave. Marshall, Michigan 49068
www.800publishing.com

PRINTED IN THE UNITED STATES OF AMERICA

Rethinking why and how we live by the way we say farewell to those we love

By Karl E. Jennings
CEO, Borek Jennings Funeral Homes
&
Co-Founder Healing Farewell Centers of America

Acknowledgments

To my wife, Kathleen, your love and sacrifices made this possible.

To my sons, Zachary, Joshua and Lukas, my heart bursts with an uncontainable joy and pride just hanging out with you.

To my parents, Ken and Arloa, you taught me to be true to myself and unrelenting in the face of adversity.

To Bill and Wilma Bullard, you are the word that became flesh and dwelled with me.

To Todd Borek, it is finished, let's get started!

To the family of Doug Baum, remembering his constant encouragement and contagious enthusiasm

To Jesus, thank you for finding me as a teenager and showing me the love that multiplies throughout the ages.

www.healingfarewellcenter.com

Preface

"What do you do for a living?" Unless you are a funeral director, you may never know what it feels like to answer this routine introductory question. Perhaps only proctologists or male gynecologists experience similar feelings. I say this because, while I don't have a problem with being a funeral director, many people I meet for the first time seem uncomfortable with my profession. With "funeral director" representing many different things to people, I never have the luxury of a predictable response. While I have heard the same jokes many times, I do wish I had a dime for every time someone said, "Boy, I bet people are just dying to meet you!"

There was a time when I had thoughts of dread about the profession in which I've been privileged to serve for more than three decades. The local morticians in the town where I grew up were the Roberts brothers. Though I came to learn later in life they were wonderful men, as a boy they were creepy to me. Reflecting on this many years later taught me that people's attitudes and ideas about my profession mirror the feelings they have about death and, not far beneath the surface, their understanding of life.

My thoughts of dread were perpetuated by the loss of my grandparents, a close friend who was killed in a car accident at the age of 18, and the death of my beloved Little League baseball coach, Mr. Sullens. I will share some of each of these experiences later in the book. It wasn't until I met Jim Van Dyke, an uncle of a young woman I was dating my sophomore year at Adrian College, that I began to reconsider my thoughts.

When I met Jim, his personality alone shredded my preconceived notions of a mortician. He laughed easily, had a joyful disposition, and was genuinely interested in helping others. From him I learned what the profession was really like and of its potential for making a significant difference in people's lives. At the time, he was working on a program that assisted children with their feelings of loss. I would later learn this made Jim exceptional in our profession; his insight was anything but commonplace within the larger industry. The potential to help people at a difficult time in their lives captured my interest. Within two years of meeting Jim, I had graduated from Wayne State University School of Mortuary Science, was working at a funeral home, and beginning to learn how people felt about death by their response to hearing what I do for a living. I was also discovering how people felt about my industry.

Consumer skepticism about the funeral industry for the past quarter century has rightfully challenged the prevailing value of the merchandise and services provided by funeral homes. In the old paradigm, funeral homes heavily weighted their prices and profit in merchandise items like caskets, vaults, and monuments. The good, better, best method of retail merchandising cemented in the consumer's mind that buying a funeral was a retail transaction equivalent to purchasing a car or appliance. This implication was to draw them to the false conclusion that the more they loved Mom or Dad, the more they'd spend on their casket.

This practice was and is exploitive; it has served to cast a pall of suspicion over the industry. More tragic, though, is that this practice blinded the best and brightest in the funeral industry to what consumers need and want. Decades have been lost and millions of dollars wasted on maximizing a retail sale instead of meeting real human needs. The funeral is a therapeutic and interactive tool for the living to begin healing. By making it a retail transaction based on feelings family members have for the dead, the industry lost the moral authority required to be trusted by a vulnerable public.

During this time, the funeral industry created an adversarial experience for those who didn't select their "traditional" services. Distracted, defensive, desperate for relevance, and faced with eroding, profitability the industry has wasted critical time, effort, and energy, paralyzed by a client base that was more and more frequently rejecting their existing service model. Finally, this state of paralysis ensured they would fail to develop the tools and resources necessary for addressing the real needs of families in distress.

Years ago, these practices led me to question the value of what funeral homes do for families. For over two decades our company has helped families through the grieving and healing process. Our experience and research in this area led to the development of a model to address the emotional, relational, and spiritual needs of families. This is how we make a difference in the lives of the families we serve; we empower them with the tools necessary for a healthy grieving experience and, ultimately, healing. These tools are found in what we have termed Acute Loss Management (ALM), which is a new field of study in Thanatology.

Now, when people ask me what I do for a living my answer is simple: "I help families begin healing."

Table of Contents

Introduction

I began my career in Ann Arbor, Michigan. Ann Arbor is a Big Ten university town and, like many young professionals who lived there, I drove a foreign car, falsely believing a foreign car meant you were not a "pedestrian consumer." In a town that doesn't consider much to be taboo, being pedestrian was the ultimate social faux pas. I would soon learn that, for many, funerals were just another pedestrian purchase.

In the early 1980s I drove a '72 Volvo Station Wagon. When I made my non-pedestrian buy, I didn't consider the commonly known fact that foreign car repair was expensive. Every time something broke I would hear my father's words, "Karl, you have champagne taste on a beer pocketbook," echo in my ears. Seems he didn't care about "pedestrian consumerism!"

It was a summer day when the blower motor stopped working in the Volvo. I went to the repair shop and was told it would cost $700 to repair, with $550 in labor costs alone. The car only cost $2K so I decided to hold off on the repair. There was really no problem in waiting, just the inconvenience of having to roll down the windows whenever the temperature rose above 75 degrees. I reminded myself that when I was a kid my only option for cooling off in a warm car was manual crank windows. Besides, it allowed me to postpone the costly repair until late fall. On the first cold autumn day I couldn't keep the frost off my windows, I decided the blower had to be fixed. Thinking the money could be better spent elsewhere, I opted to forego the expert repair and fix it myself with the help of a friend.

We began working on the car at 8:00 a.m. on a cool fall Saturday in a friend's unheated pole barn. In the following 13 hours I would come to understand the meaning of unibody construction in intimate detail. For the novice, unibody construction means that one piece is connected to the next, which in turn is connected to another and so on until it seems that every piece is connected to another. In the face of this enormous challenge, tagging and labeling each piece we removed was essential. By thc time we finished replacing the blower motor (which had been in full view for about 12 hours), the steering wheel, clutch, brake, and accelerator were the only pieces of the car that were still operational. We then replaced the motor and prepared to reassemble.

Reassembly took just a couple of hours, and we soon were inserting the key into the ignition to check that all the components had been connected properly. Turning on the fan switch engaged the blower motor; we were happy and relieved. We then flipped the switch for the emergency lights and the back windshield wiper started. As it sloshed back and forth, I wondered how much I could get for the car and sold it two weeks later.

This story highlights how I've witnessed families attempt to change their rituals and construct new paradigms for coping with death. Having no instruction book to consult, and choosing not to afford expert assistance, many people make it up as they go, at a time when they often are ill-equipped to do so.

Death and the rituals surrounding the dead are subjects few people discuss. When they do, conversation usually is limited to what to do with the remains of the deceased, who have directed their family to bury or cremate their body. In my Volvo story that would be akin to rolling down the windows. While it worked for a season, it didn't address the real issue; it only postponed the inevitable necessity of dealing with the matter, and my "fix" ended up costing more in the long run.

Though we live in a society that craves information, many face the death of a loved one with ignorance and fear. This fear is expressed the first time I am contacted by a family member with phrases like "Karl, my dad just died and I have no idea what to do" or "I just can't believe he's gone." I've heard these phrases hundreds of times by someone looking to me for guidance when faced with the death of a loved one.

After three decades of observing families endeavor to manage this difficult life experience, I wanted to provide an instructional manual that would guide them on how to cope with their loss in a way that fosters a healthy grieving experience and, ultimately, healing. This book is the result.

In the book I will be introducing a new term to Thanatology; this term is Acute Loss Management (ALM). ALM is comprised of seven phases of loss that create a foundation for a healthy grieving experience.

Seven Phases of Loss:

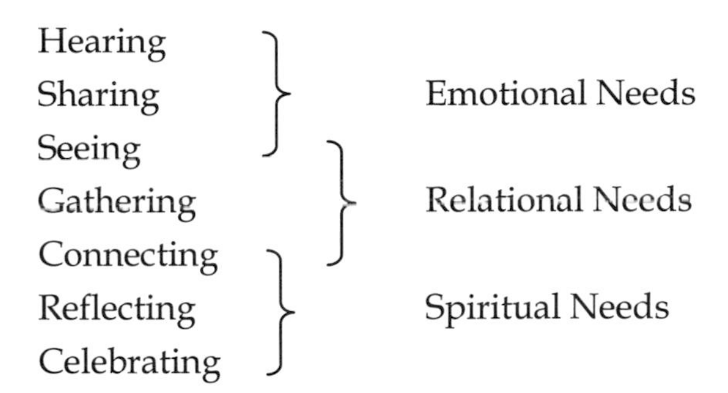

ALM is most effective when begun in the first 10 days of hearing the news of the death. It is a new way to explore, understand, and attend to the physical, emotional, relational, and spiritual needs of those experiencing loss and the role caregivers may fill in assisting the grieving. It is a discipline that is both science and art. This book will address the art of caring for, coaching, and empowering those facing life's greatest challenge and mystery. My hope is that this book will help families facing the death of a loved one and assist caregivers and clergy who will support them throughout that process.

Finally, this book is for my profession. It is time for us to join the healing professions. It is time and this is the pathway. A physician, whose daughter had committed suicide, commented to me, "You are healers, as much as any nurse or doctor I've ever dealt with; you helped us begin healing." What she references is a path to professional relevancy and the future of our beloved profession. What people want and what they need is an opportunity to begin healing. What funeral directors have to offer is experience with grieving and the opportunity to guide the grieving toward healing, which is far more valuable than a wood casket or metal vault. Please read this book with an open heart and mind and let it serve as a blueprint for your future.

Chapter 1: The Matter of Life and Death

When Death speaks...

It usually begins with a phone call from a close family member or friend. Knowing someone will die and actually hearing that it has occurred are two completely different emotional events. Even when one has been prepared that someone will die soon, as with a terminal illness, the news of the death is still received as an abrupt ending.

The almost universal response to the news is, "I can't believe they're gone." Hearing that a loved one has died hits our heart and forms a lump in our throat. It's a wound on the inside without a bruise to the body; the physiology of the body begins to respond and tears are often not far behind. The more unexpected and traumatic the loss, the more intense the physical response to it will be. A deep emotional attachment to the deceased further intensifies our physical response. For some who have had a tragic but repressed trauma earlier in life, the death of a loved one may cause unprocessed feelings to emerge. This can be both overwhelming and frightening as the survivor begins to manage both losses at once.

Our emotional attachment is the central issue we are processing when we hear the news that someone we love has died. The closer and deeper our emotional attachment to someone, the more significant the physical response to their loss will be. The physical response to the news is a manifestation of the initial stages of emotional processing. The emotional response to this news is a combination of fear, sadness, confusion, and denial. These emotions are normal, healthy, and unavoidable. You may attempt to suppress them, but that strategy will only cause a delay and further affect your physical and emotional well-being.

Attempts to quiet and steady oneself to this disorienting news are a common reaction. Because the internal response can be so intense, many immediately begin to try to suppress their external response. This is often viewed as one being "strong" for others or taking the news "well." These external reactions betray the internal feelings. This often begins a moment-to-moment battle to contain feelings we fear may cause complete collapse if permitted to be externalized. The key to a healthy loss experience is to allow our senses to become as fully engaged as possible, as soon as possible. Repressed feelings always find a release; the only question is whether that release will be healthy or unhealthy for the one grieving.

Our ears are the physical funnel through which much information reaches us. When we hear of the death of a loved one, it goes beyond the sound generated from tiny bones and nerves within our inner ear. The kind of hearing associated with hearing of the loss of a loved one passes through to the brain like a tsunami overwhelming the shore; it surges to our heart and crashes like the sudden impact of a large sledgehammer on glass.

Our brain responds like a soldier stunned by a loud, nearby explosion. Almost immediately, the heart receives the news and snaps the brain out of its temporary amnesia. In the next instant our abdomen clenches as our torso receives the news. A surge of energy swells within the body, which, unable to contain the buildup, purges tears from our eyes and moans from our voice. This kind of hearing cries for understanding from one we know fully and who knows us fully. We cannot keep this to ourselves; isolation in moments as these is disorienting and disfiguring to the soul.

I was seven years old when I first felt this way. The news that my grandfather, Russell Jennings, had died reached our family via a long distance telephone call from a relative. I didn't see Grandpa very often; he lived in Negaunee, Michigan (the Upper Peninsula or U.P.), which was about a ten-hour drive from our home in Michigan's Lower Peninsula. Grandpa Jennings was fun, loud, and happy. He made each of his grandchildren feel special and I loved him dearly.

The day I heard the news of his death is etched on my heart. In our home, my bedroom was directly across the hall from the kitchen, which was the room where our telephone was located. We only had one, and unlike modern technology, it was attached to a wall and had a short cord. It was common for me as a child to leave my door ajar and fall asleep to the sound of the conversation that took place there. The kitchen was the hub of activity for most in the mid-1960s and we were no exception.

One evening I heard the telephone ring. I peeked around my bedroom door and saw my mom pick up the receiver. She handed it to Dad who, not realizing the purpose of the call, addressed the caller with his customary and U.P.-original salutation, "How the hell are you?"

In a world of wireless communication, unlimited minutes, and favorite fives, it may be difficult for some to understand that back then long distance telephone calls were placed only for very special reasons. The joy that accompanied them was made sweeter by their infrequency. The greeting was another way of saying, "Gee, it's great to hear your voice; thank you for making me feel important and spending your money on a call to me." I think I was fifteen when I made my first long distance call. In many ways it was a right-of-passage to adulthood.

Pressing ever closer to the door I listened in, excited that someone from far away was calling, anticipating good news. I will always remember Dad's face and that a man seldom at a loss for words had none. I started crying just from seeing his response (and hearing his lack of), knowing something was terribly wrong. Then he told my mom, "Dad died." Grandpa Jennings had a stroke and had died earlier that evening. I ran to my bed, buried my face in the pillow, and cried my heart out. There are many "firsts" in life, but few have a greater impact than the first time you hear someone you love has died.

After Dad hung up the telephone, my mom gave him a hug, and then they called us children together to tell us that Grandpa Jennings had passed. My parents flew home to Negaunee for the funeral. Flying was a big deal then. A young family with a single breadwinner didn't waste money on that kind of luxury, but this event was so significant that there was no question about it; they would fly. I remember us driving to the airport and watching them board the plane. Their need to get there soon was understandable; the decision not to include us children, though common then, was not.

Children at that time were often shielded from death and grieving. Most adults project their fear and discomfort about death onto their children; children have no preconceived notions on how to react and therefore take clues from the adults around them. When children see adult family members openly grieving without proper context or reason, many will wonder if they did something wrong to make mommy, daddy, or grandma so upset. Reassuring words will help, but allowing children to participate in the grieving process can help to identify and remove false feelings of responsibility.

Because my sisters and I didn't attend the funeral, Grandpa Jennings's death was never made real to me, and I would often forget he was dead. I've been told about the same experience from others who did not participate in a funeral ritual for a friend or loved one. Each time I'd forget I would feel badly and a little ashamed, as if I betrayed his importance to my dad.

The consequence of not attending the funeral lingered for many years, as memories of Grandpa Jennings were shrouded by the experience of hearing of his death but not participating in his farewell. Without the time and place to begin the process together, each member of our family grieved in isolation. It would be years before we would talk about his life and our memories of him. By that time, Grandma Jennings had begun her descent into the fog of Alzheimer's disease. Never as warm, fun, or approachable as Grandpa, communication with Grandma was further complicated by the Alzheimer's. Memories of him faded with her memory. I would learn more of who he was from my dad, the youngest of his four sons.

How Life answers...

Death is an unwelcome visitor that many attempt to ignore. The problem is we cannot. I have been on the receiving end of this kind of news on only a few occasions and understand why people would choose to avoid any confrontation with death or the dead if they could do so. The most noble and enlightened among us struggle with thoughts of smallness, hypocrisy, shallowness, and the finite nature of life. This is not a judgment of others, but an observation from witnessing, for more than three decades, people begin to assess their own lives when coping with the death of someone else. Nothing I know of will expose the frailty of one's life with more precision than the unexpected death of a loved one.

However, the passing of a loved one provides a teachable life lesson; it is an opportunity to deal with the fear and heaviness of death. Failure to do so will only postpone, delay, and perhaps prevent connecting with others about the things that really matter in our lives. Death can serve as a catalyst to reconsider, reevaluate, and recommit to the important things in life; it presents an opportunity to confirm, discover, or authenticate that which provides meaning and significance to life.

Diminishing the depth of our pain in loss diminishes the depth of our capacity to give and receive love in life. Grieving is the price we pay for loving. Failure to grieve reduces our capacity to invest in love. We don't have funerals to dispose of bodies; we have funerals to begin a healthy grieving experience. We do this so we may love deeper, experience joy more completely, and know in its totality the beauty found in the temporal, finite moments we share on earth with those who call us "friend" and with those who call us "family." So, in the end, your death does not belong to you; it belongs to anyone who ever cared for or loved you.

Loss is painful whether our relationship with the deceased is good or bad. If our relationship was good, we have lost something that has shaped our lives for the better. If it was bad, we have lost forever an opportunity to make our relationship with them good. How we respond when we hear this news is a direct reflection of a fulfilled relationship or an unfulfilled relationship and is disorienting for opposite reasons. One longs for what they lost and the other longs for what they never had. Either way, our journey to healing begins with a word or realization that what we've known is no longer.

Hearing the news that someone we loved has died brings a permanent end to all that is good or bad about our relationship with them. Regardless of which is the more dominant, a time must be set and a place must be made to begin the framework for understanding the meaning of their life and the lessons we will carry forward from knowing them, if we are to begin healing.

Chapter 2:
The Unguarded Moment

Though I have practiced the art of acute loss management for more than two decades, my first attempts to compile universal phases about loss and healing began on September 11, 2001. I, like most Americans, found myself completely unprepared for what I call "The Unguarded Moment."

– Hearing –

It was a beautiful September day; the sun was brilliant and a cloudless blue sky blanketed the horizon. It was the type of day I hated as a school-aged child, because I would rather have been roaming my neighborhood looking for my buddies instead of suffocating inside a classroom. On this day, a friend and I were driving to a business meeting in Lansing, Michigan.

My mind was beginning to focus on the upcoming meeting as I enjoyed the scenery of rolling farms that lined the 40-mile stretch between Brighton and Lansing. For me, "Pure" Michigan is never purer than on a late summer day. My cell phone rang; it was my business partner, Todd Borek. A morning phone call was business as usual, what followed was not.

Todd said, "Karl . . . a plane has just hit the World Trade Center!"

When delivering bad news to someone we care about, most people begin this awful task with a gesture of personal attachment. It may be our first name, as my business partner had used, or a pet name, nickname, or familial title. I remember, when hearing news of Grandfather Mitchell's death, my father said, "Son, Grandpa passed away this morning." Without knowing it, he was reassuring me with this title as he tells me I no longer have a grandfather.

Dad didn't, and still does not, use that title often. But every time I hear it I'm reminded of a special bond we share. It is a title that reminds me of his love, sacrifice, and pride. As a father of three boys, it reminds me of the bond I share with each of them. They are my sons as I am my father's son.

The first word and its inflection usually alert us that something has occurred. It is one of the subconscious ways we remind those who are closest to us that we are still connected, still cared for, and still secure; and this comfort is the bridge by which bad news is delivered. When I receive bad news from someone who has little attachment to me, I feel no comfort or connection. The "awful" is complicated by feelings of insecurity and an anxious need to connect with those I care for and who care for me.

Before I could form a response, Todd repeated, "Karl, a plane has just hit the World Trade Center." I didn't respond because, like many, I couldn't respond. My mind raced. What? How could that happen? Was it pilot error? Did the pilot have a heart attack and lose control of the plane?

My first question to Todd was, "Are you sure?"

Somberly and emphatically he answered, "Yes, I saw it on TV. It's on all the networks. It is definitely a plane; it looks like it was a big one too!"

"What are they saying about how it happened?" I asked.

He replied, "They don't know . . . wait a second . . . Oh, no! The other Tower was just hit!"

I, along with millions of Americans, was not prepared for what we were hearing; our minds, souls, and hearts were unguarded. Our feelings of that day will be comparable to when we hear the news that someone we love has died.

I heard the news, yet I could not believe it. I was still in my car, the scenery I had been admiring was unchanged, but my mind was racing. My children were still at home with my wife eating their breakfast and getting ready to play with "Thomas the Train." I no longer wanted to go to my business meeting; I wanted to be home with them. I wanted to hold them and be held. I wanted my wife with me. I worried about my parents and other relatives. I wondered if anyone I knew was flying that day or in New York. Fortunately, breathing remains involuntary in moments such as these, and only those who have suffered great loss can understand the significance of that fact.

The racing in my mind was subdued as an even more intimidating fear began to wedge its way into my being, an anxiety that centered on questions about whether life would ever be the same. Had I known at the time it would remain, I would have resisted the fear much more feverishly.

– Sharing –

Within two minutes of hearing the news about the second plane, I called my wife to share what I knew. This was my first attempt to cope and regain my bearings. I asked her if she needed me to come home. She responded, "Not yet but stay in touch." I went to my meeting to find 20 people crowded together in a small room watching the events of that day being reported on TV. No one was speaking.

– Seeing –

It was in that room that I saw for the first time the magnitude of the attack on the Towers and saw the report of the attack on the Pentagon. Then we heard the report of the unknown and uncommon heroes battling in the sky for the slightest chance of saving themselves from certain death and, in doing so, protecting our homeland from another attack.

The people gathered in that small room treated it as a sanctuary and seldom spoke. When they did, comments were limited to disbelief, anger, and fear. We were trying to process what it would mean to the country, to the economy, to our children, and to our grandchildren.

In an unguarded moment the façade of safety and the illusion of security were stripped from us. We gathered around computers and TV screens in cafe's, lunchrooms, boardrooms, and schools. The world was changing; what seemed permanent was reduced to transient and what had been viewed as commonplace became restricted.

– Gathering –

That night we gathered in our homes and watched President Bush address us from the White House. He spoke from a familiar place that reminded us that not everything had changed. If he was not afraid of the terrorists, perhaps we shouldn't be afraid.

My wife and I gathered with neighbors that evening and beheld the empty sky. This scene was undoubtedly repeated across America as many neighbors were speaking to each other for the first time or connecting more personally than they had prior to

September 11. We had become a country of the "No Fly Zone." We spoke of the stillness of the sky and our pride in America. We spoke of the historic greatness of our country. We spoke of our fears. What would come next? How would we face more attacks? What kind of attack could reach us? Where would we go if we could no longer stay in our homes? These are the questions that lurked beneath the security of the familiar in all of our lives. These are questions we Americans were not accustomed to having thrust upon us so suddenly and put in such stark terms. When we experience acute loss, these are the fears and questions that race through our minds, even if they are products of a vicious cycling between our imagination and anxiety.

– Connecting –

There were noticeable changes in the weeks immediately following September 11, 2001. Attendance at religious services swelled. Americans began to reflect on what we had taken for granted or completely ignored. For the first time since the assassination of President John F. Kennedy, we were confronted with an event that stunned and united us; the labels of White, Black, Republican, Democrat, Conservative, Liberal, etc. became irrelevant; we were all just Americans. In public discourse, for the only time in my adult life, "we" became more important than "I."

– Reflecting –

Though life returned to a normal routine long ago, I have been brought to tears many times since that day. When I see an

American flag flying, I see in its shadow the ruins of the World Trade Center. When a fire truck or police car passes by, I am reminded of the rescuers going into the Towers that awful day. Seeing a priest reminds me of one who was praying over the dead before he joined them. Watching an airplane in the sky reminds me of freedom. When holding my cell phone, I wonder if someday this will be the means by which those I love will hear my final affections. Seeing a smoke cloud on the horizon makes me question if it is happening again. Anything that reminds us may provoke feelings that return us to the time we first heard the awful news.

One of my sons was born six months to the day after September 11, 2001. He knows nothing of what happened that day. My twins were born in 1998. It was explained in their history class, but they have no conscious memory of the event. Even with the history lessons, my sons will never fully comprehend the enormity of the terrorist act and the collective pain, fear, and anger felt by Americans. You had to hear, see, share, gather, and connect firsthand. Nor will they understand how the firsthand witnesses were forever changed after reflecting on the events of that day.

– Celebrating –

My sons sometime wonder why I cry when we go to a parade and I see the local American Legion or VFW group march. They will stand next to me patting me on the shoulder, encouraging me not to be sad. I didn't do this before September 11; I haven't stopped since.

Tears fill my eyes as I think of those who died on a beach in Normandy, in a rice field in Korea, or in the jungles of Vietnam; and my heart aches thinking of their stolen futures and all that life may have held for them. The men and women who march remember.

They remember not just the event of war or the occasion of battle, but the faces and names of those who died and with them their hopes, dreams, and fears. They speak to their fallen brothers' parents, siblings, wives, and girlfriends. A fleeting moment of uncommon valor, outright fear, sheer rage, or bad luck combined to produce a hero. Those who returned will tell you that the real heroes are those who were permanently maimed or didn't make it home.

My heart fills with gratitude for today's service men and women who leave their families and risk their lives to protect my family and me, to keep our homeland safe, and to protect our right to live free. I really don't know how to honor them for their sacrifice; there are no words or tributes that adequately match their sacrifice. So, as I wipe away tears of pride and sadness, I applaud them.

When celebrating the things that matter most, it is possible to be both grateful and sad. The death of a cherished friend or family member will cause us to consider the things that matter most in our lives. A profound experience of grief and healing will expand our appreciation of those around us and things we may have taken for granted up to that day.

My family is fortunate to watch the parade and build memories. The children of those who served and sacrificed may be at the same parade on this same street for the same occasion; their memories will be different.

The summer of 2002 our family vacationed at a cottage located on the eastern edge of the beautiful Lake Michigan shoreline. I used part of this vacation time for spiritual renewal and retreat. It had been eleven months since the attacks. As I looked across the lake at a majestic sunset, a masterpiece painted by Nature began to unfold and be recreated again and again with the slow lowering of the sun, which all too soon dissolved into the horizon. In the stillness of this evening I counted my blessings; I finished several hours later. I had exhausted myself, but not the list of things for which I was grateful. I had never done this before, and never had I experienced such an overwhelming gratitude for even the most subtle gifts I'd been given. The year since the previous September 11 was a time of reflection and of taking account of the things that mean the most to me: life, love, family, faith, friends, and community.

From Gift Receiver to Gift Giver

The listing of my blessings may have stopped with the setting sun, but I felt a sincere and persuasive pull to live differently. I wanted to be vital. I did not want to go quietly, fearfully, and humbly into the future; I wanted to live with intention, be engaged, overcome obstacles, tackle bigger challenges, and make a difference.

If the voices of Normandy could speak, would they say, "Go timidly into the dark night which is death." I suspect not. No, they would say, "Charge the beach, run hard, breathe deep, and don't wait until your last day on this earth to live fully."

When confronting the finite nature of life, I'm compelled to be a better father, husband, leader, and citizen. These are so similar to the feelings I had while fondly gazing at my grandfather, Cyril Mitchell, while he lay in his casket and I wondered about my life. Would it measure up to the standard he had set? Would I run the course of life with the dignity and grace of a proud Englishman who, as a young boy, became an even prouder American?

When the world changes as it did on September 11, 2001, the depth or the shallowness of our life is exposed. In some form or another we ask, "If I had died that day, would I have died before learning how to live?" The things that matter the most in life step to the forefront and the trivial are made transparent. Healing begins when we embrace that which matters the most in life by integrating it into our present.

There is only one other way we experience this in life, and it usually begins with a phone call. A call telling you that someone you dearly love has just died.

Chapter 3: Acute Loss Management

A Brief Overview

– Hearing –

We were standing in the entryway of the cafeteria at Bair Lake Bible Camp when Shari, my girlfriend at that time, was summoned to the telephone at the other end of the building. Shari and I had met at college. She volunteered during the summer as a camp counselor, and I would come down to the camp on weekends to help with maintenance projects. We had been dating for a little over two years, and during that time, I had met most of her close-knit family. News of any kind traveled quickly in this family. Within seconds of picking up the telephone, her entire body deflated and she immediately began to shake and cry. I ran across the room and arrived as she was hanging up. As I embraced her, she said her cousin Kimberly was dead. It was several minutes before any more words were spoken.

The details of Kimberly's death came out over the next hour. It happened on a family trip at the hotel where they were staying. A lifeguard ran an electrical cord through the opening of a sliding metal door that served as access between two pools. Closing the door severed the cord and Kim was killed when she touched the door. The more the story was repeated, the more unbelievable it became. A sudden death such as Kimberly's is the origin of a myriad of questions about timing, fate, and "what if" scenarios that will repeat in the minds of the family over and over again without ever being completely resolved.

Kimberly was only twelve and was very bright. She was loved deeply and her life was full of promise. Kim lived in a nurturing community that provided her shelter and a safe haven; it is where grandparents, playmates, siblings, teachers, aunts, uncles, and cousins interacted regularly and sometimes daily.

In the immediate moments after the news of Kim's death had reached Shari, a gaping hole was left in her community as those who had loved, played, taught, cuddled, laughed, and cried with her had to imagine their lives without her.

With a tragedy such as this, the pain is incomprehensible, as it should be. If it were something we were able to comprehend, it is doubtful we would ever risk loving. This kind of tragedy forces us to analyze all that is glorious about life, love, and living. Accepting such acts as the will of God leaves many not liking God much. Accepting them as an act of fate leaves one with an endless stream of questioning and a permanent feeling of vulnerability to pain that if repeated could kill you; this is something only those who have had the experience can understand.

In the end, one is resigned to accepting what occurred because it is a fact and the pursuit of asking "Why?" seems endless. Acceptance doesn't mean one has fully understood or even made peace with their loss. Acceptance means that one realizes that they will now live with questions, doubts, and frustrations that may never be satisfied.

What makes this tragedy even worse is that parents lose not only a child, but also suffer the symbolic loss of the many events they expected to share with that child such as birthdays, graduations, wedding, and the births of their grandchildren. The milestone dates and events are always acknowledged, whether silently or aloud.

Life goes on, it has to for the parents and for their other children, and so does the heartache.

– Sharing –

It is not long before the Hearing Phase merges with the Sharing Phase. Sharing begins when we share the news of our loss with someone else. Usually, it is with the person closest to us, who cares about us the most, or the person nearest in proximity. It may be a spouse, child, parent, or co-worker; it most often is someone in our closest circle of friends and family. We share with those we can be the most vulnerable with and know will be the most supportive. After the first words are spoken, it is not uncommon to sit quietly together, recalling stories, and thinking of others (family members, friends, clergy, etc.) who also need to be told.

Sharing in the early stage of loss is our attempt to inform others and also begins the journey of engaging them with our feelings. Sharing will set the habit of opening up about the loss and provides the context of one's feelings to friends. In sharing our thoughts and emotions, we begin to build the emotional support system that will carry us through the months of our grief long after others have returned to their lives and activities. Involving others at the time of the loss allows us to engage them in the future, long after the loss, and keeps us from becoming isolated in our grief. Without sharing, the grieving process can force people into isolation with the false belief that no one understands or cares.

It also benefits the people sharing in the loss. The further removed someone is from the loss, the more impatient they may appear to be with the grieving person. Not only does sharing alleviate the impatience, it allows them to connect and remain connected. Maintaining that bridge of comfort where both feel connected, cared for, and secure can be beneficial for dealing with the loss immediately and in the long term.

It's important to realize that, for some of your friends, experiencing your grief is a reminder of their own feelings of loss that haven't been fully understood or resolved. You may find yourself in conversation with them talking about a loss that took place years earlier. Just remember, grieving doesn't have a timetable.

Others may make insensitive or even clueless remarks, such as "It's for the best" or "You'll get over it with time." It is, therefore, important to share your thoughts with those who can listen without judgment. This can be a complex maze to maneuver and an extra portion of grace is often required at a time when simply managing the immediate affairs of life can be overwhelming. When sharing your feelings in this early stage of loss, identify those who can listen and those who cannot. Be generous to both, but only seek counsel with the willing and sensitive.

The message here should be clear; you set the pattern for sharing your feelings from the outset of hearing the news that someone you love has died. Providing a time and place to share your feelings with both those who share in your loss and those who are friendly participants is essential to healthy grieving and the process of healing.

– Seeing –

The Sharing Phase is followed by the Seeing Phase. As your friends hear for the first time that your loved one has died, they will begin to share that news with others. One of the first questions they will ask is, "When will the services be held?" They ask it in those words, but what they really want to know is when and where they are going to be able to see you. It is important to understand that 70 percent of the people who attend a funeral will not have known the deceased. They will come to see you, pay respects to your loved one, and let you know that you matter to them. Seeing you will help to make your loss real to them and provide the opportunity to share memories of your loved one's life. They will share in both your loss and your memories.

Seeing the deceased for the first time makes their death real. The phrase "seeing is believing" is never truer than when seeing a deceased loved one. This is the emotional level setter for everyone in the family.

After they hear of the loss, family members often quickly move from an emotional response to practical planning. They may be separated by hundreds of miles and have to deal with the logistics of getting back home to attend the funeral, on top of planning the service itself, all while their emotions run high and their thoughts are racing. After arriving home, they walk in the door to see and greet other members of their family; it can feel similar to any other family gathering.

It is only when they see the deceased at the funeral home, standing with those who grieve the death, that they are confronted with the reality of what has taken place. They have moved from emotionally reacting and logistically planning to reality.

Seeing is what puts everyone all at the same emotional level; seeing makes it real.

Our minds are informed throughout our lives by our senses. Our senses must be included in the loss experience for the mind to be fully informed and prepared to begin healing. When we see the dead we begin to inventory our losses. This is painful because we realize all that we shared is now part of history and memories. We see the decedent's deceased face, no expression. We look at their eyes, no connection. We touch their hand, no response. We cry soulfully, they are unmoved. We know only in part when we hear the news that someone has died. When we see them dead, we know more fully. Healing can begin only as one accounts for what has been lost.

Many disparage the viewing of the dead as unnecessary and even barbaric. However, most instinctively understand the importance. Consider the families of the fallen soldier, murder victim, or those lost in the terrorist attacks and what they wouldn't give for the body of their loved one. Think of the money spent on finding and identifying remains.

Recently, the body of a Vietnam veteran was identified and returned to his family after nearly 40 years. One family member described the funeral service as more of a homecoming. Ritual with the soldier's body present provided the family proof of his death and comfort in knowing he was where he belonged. Finally, the family explained, they have closed an open wound.

– Gathering –

The Seeing Phase is followed by the Gathering Phase. The first part of this phase may begin with extended family gathering at a family member's home or at the funeral home. Eventually, this will move to the arrangement conference and continue to expand as you progress through this phase of your loss. The old adage "we only get together for weddings and funerals" is true. Between the two, most believe only funerals are mandatory. At this time you will see relatives you may not have seen in years. They share your loss because they share your heritage and are a part of your family legacy. It will come as no surprise that not everyone will agree on the choices that were made. Because of this, it is important to remember that there is no right way or wrong way to say farewell. Each person's needs are unique and ought to be valued by others.

The gathering phase is a busy time marked by a list of items that require attention, such as working with the funeral home to attend to the details of the service, managing the affairs of the family, early phone calls from friends, collecting personal memorabilia, ordering flowers, planning the luncheon, and meeting with your clergy.

Gathering the things you will share and taking time for making these arrangements allows you to make the smoothest possible transition from hearing the initial news to preparing yourself to greet others. Having a day or so will aid in preparing to engage others. Most need this time practically and emotionally as they begin to reorient to life without their loved one. Be patient with yourself and others at this time . . . well-meaning people can make some pretty dim-witted comments in their attempts to console.

– Connecting –

The Gathering Phase is followed by the Connecting Phase. This can be the most emotional, challenging, and rewarding phase of the farewell experience. People want to let you know they share your loss and need direction from you on how to do this. One of the most effective ways to connect with extended family and friends is to bring memorabilia from the person's life to a visiting time. Providing an opportunity to visit is really just creating a time and place to connect others to memories; to receive and offer love and support from those closest to us; and enable others to share in our loss.

The Connecting Phase is a powerful way of reminding us in the midst of loss that life will go on, and that we are not alone and will not be abandoned. Failure to plan for a time and place for connecting indirectly suggests that you do not wish to share your loss, and that can be viewed as a "no trespassing" sign. As such, friends will not know when, where, or how to interact with you. When they see you at the grocery store, post office, or church they will not know if it's okay to express their sympathy and concern, or if doing so will frustrate or sadden you.

By making a time and place to connect with others, you control how, when, and where you are willing to share this experience. Failure to provide that time and place relinquishes to others the control of how, when, and where they will interact with you.

– Reflecting –

The Connecting Phase slowly segues to the Reflecting Phase. You and those who gather and connect will naturally begin to reflect on the meaning and significance of the life shared with your loved one. As your loved one's life stories are told, your memories will lead you to a place of reflection about their life and your own. How did they impact or influence you? What would life have been like without them? What will I tell my children about this person? How do I want to be like them? For what am I most grateful?

For most, this is a time of life review and can be a transformational experience for many. People who have made poor choices in their lives or postponed painful decisions will often use this opportunity to change their personal habits and behaviors. I've seen survivors lose 50 pounds of excess weight, quit smoking, leave abusive marriages, recommit to failing marriages, forgive a relative or friend, or change their career direction. The life review that occurs at the time of death is profound for many and will need time to fully mature. The death of a loved one shared in the context of a loving family: nurtured by a ritual that attends to emotional, relational, and spiritual needs of each person: serves as the platform for a healthy grieving experience and life transformation. During this time of reflection, usually two or three central themes of the person's life emerge from the stories shared and heard, and they need to be given expression in the Celebration Phase.

– Celebration –

It is during the celebration phase that you begin embracing both the meaning of your loved one's life and the significance of their death. It is a time to appreciate the greatest and least significant moments of your life as meaningful and a part of who you ultimately become. If you lose your way in life, celebrating those things that matter the most can remind you of what is most important and who you are. Celebration acknowledges both the significance of human loss and the value of human love. The celebration is inspiring without being festive. It is heartwarming, uplifting, and meaningful to those closest to the loss.

Our Hope

The goal of this book is to demonstrate the seven progressive phases of acute loss management that will foster healing for families and their communities at the time of loss and in the days, weeks, and months following. By demonstrating the seven phases, we hope we can take the mystery out of what to do when a loved one dies, and focus, instead, on how to maximize the benefits from each of these stages so you can grieve, grow, heal, and continue to love.

Chapter 4: Hearing

Our bodies were made to purge from us those things we should not suppress.

When I was a young man, a friend of mine was critically injured in a car accident. Upon arrival to the hospital, he was immediately rushed from the Emergency Room to surgery. I was told his father was in the waiting area when the doctors informed him that his son had died. When he heard the news, witnesses say it was as if the strength was zapped from his legs and the air removed from his lungs. He collapsed to the ground, folded into the fetal position, and after about 10 seconds, released a soulful moan.

When we hear a loved one has died, our body responds to this from the nuanced to the palpable, and the response is its attempt to say, "This news hurts, it cuts deeply." There is almost a direct correlation between the traumatic nature of what we hear and the intensity of our physical response to it.

We learn about the death from our senses; we first hear or see the event. Our auditory nerve or optic nerve processes the news and sends a message to our brain that, in turn, releases a series of messages to the rest of our body. Our emotional attachment is the central emotional issue we are processing when we hear the news that someone we love has died. The closer and deeper our emotional attachment to someone, the more significant the emotional response to their loss will be.

The science of the physical manifestation during acute stress is real, and most people understand this intuitively without evidence. There is no scientific certainty to much of what you will read in this book, except in this arena. When we receive tragic news, our bodies respond with alarm, protection, fear, uncertainty, anxiety, and all of the emotions that are a part of the reaction to acute loss.

No matter how the news of a death reaches us, the notification is almost always accompanied with an immediate physical response. Many phrases have been used to describe these sensations, such as: I felt lightheaded, it felt like a blow to my stomach, it was gut-wrenching, I couldn't stop shaking, I couldn't clear my mind, and it left me breathless. The physiological and anatomical responses to sudden tragic news are real. Tears will flow no matter how stoic we try to be. Our chins quiver, and the repetitive recoiling that expands and constricts the core of our being seems, for a moment, to be involuntary. Our bodies were made to purge from us those things we should not suppress.

It was several minutes before my friend's father could speak; when he was able, he demanded to see his son. He went into the softly lit room where his son had been brought; he reached down, taking his son's fractured head in his hands, held his son's head to his chest, and wept. He was taking his first step in healing by acknowledging, witnessing, absorbing, and concluding that his son was physically dead.

I've witnessed a mourner's need to physically engage the dead many times— from a mother who wrestles for hours unable to release her stillborn child to the hospital staff, to the spouse who sits quietly next to the bed of a lifelong love unwilling to separate. This attachment is emotional, expressed physically. This interaction is emotionally therapeutic and reflects human instincts at their most basic level. Hearing the news that someone died compels us to touch and care for our loved one and is essential to the healing process. We caress and hold them because of our love and affection for them. Unknowingly, we are confronted with their inability to do the same for us.

Those who have loved deeply are attached to the body of their loved one. They didn't love the idea of their loved one; they loved the expression of that idea in human flesh. We birth, bathe, feed, protect, embrace, and celebrate in our physical bodies. Which would you rather have the affection of, an XOXOX found at the bottom of a personal correspondence or the actual hug and kiss? While the idea of affection warms our heart, the reality made flesh engages our senses. We hear with our ears, we see with our eyes, we touch with our hands, we smell with our noses, we kiss with our lips, and we embrace with our bodies. Suddenly at death, we realize this will never happen again.

When we love and give ourselves to others, we become a part of their lives and are emotionally impacted by their successes and misfortunes. We care about the things they care about, hurt over the things that hurt them, share in their happiness, embrace their dreams, and celebrate their blessings. We integrate their story into our own: sentences, paragraphs, and chapters that forever affect the joy, meaning, and outcome of our life and happiness. When they die, so too does a part of us.

Few are fortunate enough to script an ideal scenario for their death. Few say all the things they needed to, express affections and forgiveness in their fullness, and few greet the news of death with a sense of satisfied contentment. Most survivors and decedents would like one more day, one more hug, one more smile, one more, and one more . . . just one more of what we long for. We cannot know this in its full magnitude until those we care for are forever unavailable to us.

For those who have never loved deeply, their attachment is shallow and their need to grieve the death of a loved one or allow others to grieve the death is the same. Creatures of the expedient and superficial will dispose of their dead in the same manner.

At a minimum the news that a close family member or friend has died is emotionally disorienting. The emotions that accompany this news can seem to be overwhelming; it would be very unfortunate if it were otherwise.

Several years ago, we served a family whose daughter had become progressively more addicted to harder and harder drugs. She started by smoking marijuana in 10th grade with friends who gathered at parties after various athletic events. She had been a model student: but succumbing to peer pressure and a desire to have fun, she began smoking-once a week at first. Eventually, the habit grew to once a day and then before school, during lunch, and after school. A stunning beauty, she soon began to run with a crowd that would give her what she wanted if she gave them what they desired. When they had no further use for her, she turned to the streets and lived a life that had her scavenging for food and selling her body for drugs.

Tragically, she was found dead near the church she attended as a child. She weighed less than 100 pounds. The cause of death was a lethal combination of malnutrition and drug addiction. She was 24 years old. In eight years, she went from having everything to live for, to exhausting her body of life. One of her close high school friends spoke at the funeral and directed these words to her parents, "We loved her so much. It seems like I've cried everyday for the past six years. Early on, she would still meet us, talk about her drug use, explain that it was just a phase she was going through and how she wanted to come back to school. We hoped that she would. We prayed that she would. We begged her to stop, and though I've felt brokenhearted hundreds of times before now, today I feel as if a part of me has died."

She expresses the feelings of attachment to which I'm referring. The emotional bond to her friend was integrated into the experience of her life. When her friend suffered, she suffered. When her friend dreamed, she invested in her dream and finally, when she died, she felt as if a part of her had died. Perhaps this is why it seems that the elderly no longer cling as aggressively to life. In the latter years of life, they slowly become detached, some by choice but mostly because those they knew, loved, and laughed with are gone.

When we commit to caring for another human being, sharing life's experiences with them and integrating their life experience into our own, we commit to grieve their misfortunes and death. This is why our deaths and lives do not belong to us. As this young woman said, she felt as if a part of her had died. As we age our attachments are less to people and more to our memories. This is one of the ways the soul prepares itself for life's final journey and why it's so hard for so many when the young die.

"All mankind is of one author, and is one volume; when one man dies, one chapter is not torn out of the book, but translated into a better language; and every chapter must be so translated...As therefore the bell that rings to a sermon, calls not upon the preacher only, but upon the congregation to come: so this bell calls us all: but how much more me, who am brought so near the door by this sickness....No man is an island, entire of itself...any man's death diminishes me, because I am involved in mankind; and therefore never send to know for whom the bell tolls; it tolls for thee."

John Donne

16th Century priest and lawyer

This quote illustrates ideas that emerged during the Renaissance Era. Affirming humanity by acknowledging that we are not isolated from each other but connected. This connectedness elevates the significance and value of each life in community.

Perhaps there is no more obvious sign of this connectedness than the desire to be close to those we most care about when we receive the news that someone we love has died. We remain diminished until we both fully embrace how the deceased enhanced our lives and then begin to bless others in the same way.

On Sept. 11, 2001, after I heard the second Tower had been hit, I immediately desired to call my wife and did so in a matter of seconds. Shortly after, I called my parents and siblings. I say this as a matter of reflection. I responded at the time without considering, pondering, or contemplating.

Like most that day, I was reacting. It was unfiltered, unscripted, and unplanned. This was exactly what I needed to do before I could move forward. When we are suddenly detached from the familiar, we must reach out to the secure to reestablish and reorient our bearings. When the foundation of our life is shaken, we need to assess and acknowledge what remains. This is how we first cope with tragic news.

Where were you when you first heard the news that a plane had hit the World Trade Center? Whom did you first call on Sept. 11? What did you talk about? Know that the feelings of that day will parallel the feelings you will experience when you hear the sudden or unexpected news of the death of a loved one. This helps to prepare for the pattern and reality of this experience, not to attempt to buffer or protect your response. Being unguarded for this news is a reality of the experience, being unprepared is not.

The news that someone has died leaves an instant relational void that can only be dealt with by securing contact with those who survive. If the news of the death of a loved one knocks us off balance, we reach out to those who know us to catch us and reestablish our footings. It's as if a hole is created by the loss and needs to be temporarily filled by those who remain.

Chapter 5: Sharing

Sharing is to healing as oxygen is to the body.
Without it we will shrivel up and die.

Pete opened his conference with me by stating that his mother was dying at a local hospital and he needed information to help his family plan. He said we had to hurry because she was near the end. I told him we could wait if she was indeed that close to death. "No," he said, "I want to get this over with." This was said in the context of our meeting, though it seemed intended for ending the course of dying he'd been dealing with for three weeks.

Pete was hoping for a quick conclusion to the awfulness of what was interrupting his life. If you retain anything I've written, remember this: *wanting to get this over with is not something that will happen in a one hour meeting, three days of funeral ritual, or one solid month of wishing it was over.* You get over it not by going around it, but by going through it; and anyone who tells you otherwise doesn't know what they're talking about.

We had completed about 30 minutes of the conference when my administrative manager interrupted. Pete's wife was on the telephone. You could see the blood leave his face; his hand began to shake as he picked up the phone. The only thing I heard him say was, "I'll be right there." As he stood up to leave he said, "Mom's dead. I've got to go." Concerned for his state of mind, I asked if we could drive him to the hospital. He declined and we walked to his car.

On the way out he asked, "How do you deal with this every day?"

"I don't and couldn't if I were deeply attached to everyone I served," I explained. "Your mother's death belongs to you and your family. I help those facing loss to manage and understand how they can begin to heal and help one another through this experience."

Pete left. He needed to be with his family and they needed him. The impulse to connect with those closest to us is real and profound. Knowing we are not alone provides us the confidence to endure whatever challenges we face.

Many of those who survived the horrors of prison camps during war, did so because they held hope they would be reunited with those they loved. Those who gave up, frequently did so upon hearing the news that their family had been killed. Many a solider has held some vestige of a sweetheart, a symbol of attachment to a world he longs to return to and a reminder of why he must fight. His cause is to return to those he loves. The item he carries is his attachment to them. In the initial moments of loss, it is imperative to be surrounded by those you love and who love you.

Many people have had the experience of needing to share a traumatic moment with those who are hurting, such as: rallying at the home of a friend when a child has been missing, gathering for a prayer meeting at church when catastrophe strikes somewhere in the world, contacting a friend when you've heard that they've been diagnosed with a disease, or visiting a hospital when someone is recovering from surgery. In the midst of our insecurity we find comfort in numbers and are reminded of those things in our life that are assured.

We need to share the experience with those we care about the most. It matters greatly to know in physical manifestation that people are with you. It is not enough to think or imagine their presence, anymore than one can imagine the kiss of a lover or the warm hug of a friend.

Sharing begins the caring for our emotional needs; it is our first attempt to say to others, "I need you. Please join me in this process and understand my anguish." Sharing also begins the healing process. It is where we attend to the most intimate needs of our hearts, minds, and souls. We feel most safe when we are with those who are closest to us. We are able to weep without judgment and allow our minds to wander without consequence.

Sharing is to healing as oxygen is to the body. Without it we will shrivel up and die. As we begin to connect and attend to our emotional needs and to those around us, we initiate the first in a series of moments where our hearts will be comforted by the knowledge that we have suffered a loss but are not alone.

Many people I have served tell me they did not cry until they saw a family member. They seemed to hold it together until they were in a place and with people where their reaction required no explanation. Often, in these moments, no words are exchanged; a glance will be followed by a hug that provides shelter for our tears. The tragic news that was received into their bodies now finds release, at times uncontrolled, but shared in the security of love. It's impossible to experience loss without sharing it with those close to us. Not to do so would be like taking a sharp blow to our leg without flinching in pain.

If the pain of loss is bottled inside a person, if no release is found, if no security is offered, if no consolation is given, they will experience further emotional and social distance. Sadly, for those who never have been able to be emotionally vulnerable to and with others, this is a time of stoic sadness and further relational isolation. This isolation can be falsely comforting. Not reminded of our loss and unaware of its impact on others, those who are hidden in their grief become even more detached from those who could help them the most.

The characteristics underlining this stoic sadness and relational isolation are often bitterness and self-condemnation. We see these negative behaviors emerge as those who choose no or little ritual struggle to interact with others, including those closest to them. These attributes can make those suffering loss in this way defensively offensive. They tend to be withdrawn and detached from others until offended by an action or comment. Such offense can be taken without much cause and will often be greatly disproportionate to the named cause. This is how unresolved grief works; it finds something else to attach itself to and creates responses that range from inappropriate to harmful. It is a way to push away anyone who exposes the pain of those who are desperately trying to conceal it. Emotionally healthy people in functional relationships need to and must share their most intimate feelings of loss with those closest to them. In doing so, we expose our emotional and relational needs. Initially, what is being shared is the first wound—the experience of hearing of the loss—and this wound finds its expression in the phrase "I can't believe they're gone." This must not be confused with the acceptance of the loss; we will share what the experience of hearing was like, not what the experience of loss is like.

In the moments after hearing, we share, not our grief, not even the specifics of what was lost. We share the unfolding meaning of unexpected news, and often without words. We share hugs to hold onto those who are still here and needing to feel the life they hold within their body to remind ours that we are still connected, even when words fail to coherently express our thoughts. We share emptiness without yet knowing what has been taken from us. We share our disbelief, fear, angst, helplessness, hopelessness, and numbness.

Many who hear of the death of a loved one limit their

exposure to loss to these two steps. They hear and share with a multitude of people how they responded to hearing the news. Families choosing little or no ritual at the time of death do not provide the time and place to begin inventorying the blessings and gifts given to them and others by the deceased. These gifts, from the subtle to the profound, undergird the substance of relationships and serve as the platform for building a mind-set of gratitude that is essential for a healing grief experience.

The Antidote

Hearing of the death of a loved one . . .
It's like a seed planted in the soul of our being.
We don't know what it will become, how it will grow, what it will demand of us, why it happened now…
but we know the seed is imbedded; it is taking root and will grow.
We seek out those closest to us, because without words being spoken we know the same seed was planted in them.
The urge to suppress these odd, uncomfortable, and intimidating feelings is motivated primarily by ignorance and fear.
We do not know how to deal with our feelings about death and we do not know what will come next.
What we know in the first moments after hearing is that the feelings are so intimidating and intrusive that we must fight to ignore them,
attempt to starve the seedling
or find others who are similarly afflicted.
Recognize this, the seed will survive;
like a parasite that will feed on the host
until the antidote is applied.
Sharing is the antidote and healing begins when we begin to share our feeling of loss with those we love and who love us.

Chapter 6: Seeing

The moment when the spirit made flesh becomes the flesh made spirit.

This is a painful story. It could cause you to want to hug those you love, forgive those who need your forgiveness, connect with lost family or friends, and look at each moment and person in your life differently.

It was 6:15 a.m. She lay in bed wide awake when the alarm clock rang out. Later that night was the biggest basketball game of the year between crosstown rivals. Jenny was the captain of her cheer squad, and she awoke early, unable to rest her mind from rehearsing her much anticipated moment in the spotlight.

"Jen, get up, your friends will be here in 15 minutes," a declaration from her father that was no more disrupting to her morning routine than the prompting of a snooze alarm. "I'm up and ready, Dad," she responds.

She walked into the kitchen where Dad was preparing breakfast and Mom was surfing the net. It was all normal. Her father gives her an affectionate peck on the forehead, and she runs out the door to join her friends on a ride to school.

At 7:15 a.m. she lay in her father's arms, in the back seat of her friend's car. He cradled her as he had when she was a child and as he hadn't for years. He wept and rocked her. He thought for a moment of a time when she broke her arm; she was in pain that day. Today, she is in a place without pain. Like a lightning bolt piercing the darkness of night, he realizes she is DEAD. He loses control of his emotions and time becomes meaningless. For a moment his agony is interrupted as a paramedic peers into the twisted metal tomb where the questions of when, where, and how of his daughter's future are abandoned and replaced with "Whys?" and "What ifs."

A great group of young achievers piled into a car that morning, they were more driven than driving. Excited, exuberant, and distracted one moment; breathless, blood-stained, and broken the next. As they entered the intersection, they were met by a speeding truck with a driver going too fast to a place that will leave him racked with regret, sorrow, and eventually a haunted sobriety. Fatal and fate-filled accidents are places where no query or inquiry can make sense of the senseless. Two dead, four injured, and one drunk.

When I met Jen's father, he wandered into the funeral home as if he were lost. He was. The crimson hands that cradled her hours earlier now shook mine as he thanked me for meeting with him. His hands were still unwashed four days later, when we placed her in a hill that overlooked her childhood playground.

Jen's father was sitting down to eat the breakfast he was making when she left that morning. He had heard the collision; the accident occurred just a quarter mile from their home. His wife ran for the telephone, he ran to the noise.

As he ran, the scene just outside his neighborhood unfolded as he imagined with people and cars crowding around. He couldn't see the car at first, so he thought that maybe Jen was safely on her way to school. He kept running when a friend, who was already at the scene, saw him coming and ran to met him. He said, "It's the car Jen was in. I couldn't get to her but it looks bad, really bad."

He thought, "Hurt bad? How bad. . .bad is not dead! Is it?" He notices people stare as he approaches the car. He sees the car; he sees two kids who are moving, bleeding, and lying on the road. He sees another slumped behind the steering wheel. He can't see his daughter.

When you become a parent, there seems to be a built-in radar system that enables you to constantly observe the movement of your children. He hopes to see movement that he recognizes as hers, he hopes to hear her voice and he longs to hear her cry or scream. He hears and sees nothing until he notices a charm bracelet glittering in the morning sun, her bracelet.

He dives into the car, moves debris off her body, and sees blood and bone. He tries to wipe away the blood but there's too much. He listens for a breath or a sign of breathing. . .none. He reaches for her pulse . . . none. He then sees *it.* The *it,* he will see in his mind until he no longer breathes. This is when he knows she is dead, *it* has left no doubt. *It* is what the medic sees and the reason he didn't disturb her father's grief. His body slumps and he cradles her in his arms. It would be two hours before he would be able to leave her.

When we grieve, we grieve physically first. From the time we first hear the news, to sharing it with others, our bodies are measuring, absorbing, calculating, and adjusting to the news of the death. We must see those we love to fully inform our senses that they are indeed dead. Until we fully comprehend with sight, sound, touch, and smell we can't be fully informed and, therefore, are detached from the fullness of the loss.

His wife is held back by a neighbor, this is a kindness at first. She initially accepts their restraint and is willing to let them do the thinking for her. Her neighbor is holding her when she demands to see her daughter. As she approaches the car, she sees ***it*** also. She recoils and seeks a safer place, the way Jackie Kennedy did after the second shot. This can't be happening, it must be a nightmare. This is her baby girl, her bright, bubbly, and headstrong baby girl.

"NOOO!!!" Her only words before she collapses to the ground; a paramedic aids her.

By the time Jen's father emerges from the back of the car, many family and close friends are there to buffer the transition. Her blood is on his shirt, pants, hands, arms, and shoes. Her parents then return to the house and recount the events of the day with the police, who inform them of where their daughter's body is being taken. The police officer said it exactly that way, . . . "their daughter's body." This would be the first in hundreds of well-intended comments from the clueless or careless that would at first traumatize and then anger them. He blurts, "You mean my daughter, that is my daughter!"

Before the police leave, they tell Jen's parents to contact a funeral home. It had been over three hours since the accident, and the thought of having to call a funeral home had not entered their mind. With its entry, the realization of what has happened penetrates deeper and stuns them like a hard slap on the face. Call a funeral home, for our daughter; this harshest of all realities becomes even more real and unforgiving. A family member suggests one and someone else another. He feels unprepared, ill- equipped, and now completely dependent on the counsel of a stranger. They pick up a telephone book. Our business name begins with the letter *B* so he calls us first. I answer the phone, "Thank you for calling Borek Jennings, this is Karl Jennings." His nightmare and heartache are expressed in four words, "My daughter is dead." An hour later he arrives at the funeral home: he needed to see it before he could decide. I greet him. After our visit I wrote these words.

Looking For Yesterday

The mourning begins with the intense glare of a rising sun.
Sunrise, both blinding and foreboding…
Squealing tires and crunching metal.
Panic soon consumes the soul as the horrific intersects with regret.
He'd kissed her that morning; his lips tenderly touched her forehead.
His, a paternal ritual of affection; hers, a teenager's indulgence.
Their next kiss is touched by the chilling shroud of the eternal.
"Where does the love of God go?" The Lyricist has queried
But love is not absent in this moment…
The absence of love would be kinder and gentler than this unspeakable…
He asks to see our room of repose as if looking for a place large enough to hold his grief…
Sauntering from room to room he greets each with an empty stare,
The unmistakable gaze of the hopeless and lifeless…
He inquires, "Are there other funeral homes in this town."
"Yes," I respond, "Perhaps it would be helpful to visit them."
I know, what he may never; the place he seeks belongs to yesterday,
A place he will never find and can no longer exist.

What is unfolding in this too often repeated story is simply the emotionally overwhelming impulse to be physically present with those who have died. Sitting in the back of the car, Jen's father is engaging all his senses in the moment of his daughter's death. He moves from attempting to rescue to holding the permanently broken body of his daughter.

He holds and rocks her back and forth; this motion is an instinctive byproduct of her early childhood when he would rock her to sleep or comfort her. He is being comforted now. He will likely be healthier sooner, because he was fully present and allowed himself those several minutes to absorb physically what death looks and feels like. As happiness has little meaning without the context of sadness, life without the knowledge of death is diminished. Healing without tending to the wound leaves room for the likelihood of infection.

When he sees her next, the signs of trauma will be gone. *It* will be repaired and hidden beneath her hair and carefully applied cosmetics. The bloody accident will no longer own her body, and her beauty minus the bubbly will be his last visual memory of her. Her mother will have her time then. She will twist Jen's hair gently between her fingers for what seems to be hours. She will kiss her, again and again.

They realize Jen can't feel these expressions of affection and touch. Her mother is reminded with each touch and kiss that this is what dead looks, feels, and smells like. In the softness of a velvet-lined casket the memories of smashed glass and blaring sirens seem unreal.

What is real is their daughter; she is not moving, she is still and quiet, like a baby girl taking a mid-afternoon nap. Her mother touches her arm, shakes it a little, hoping this is a bad dream and that God will perform a miracle healing and bring her child back from death and her family back from the awfulness of this moment. Soon hours have past. Hundreds of people have come to share their shock and love. They are all gone now when Mom and Dad make their way back up to the casket. They must say "goodnight" the night before the day they must say "good bye."

As they walk up to her casket, this moment prompts a memory of the bedtime routine, when they would go together to tuck their children in bed at night. At this time, they are glad they made the effort to do this and are perplexed by how to do it now. How do you say goodnight to a dead daughter, when you must say goodbye forever the next day? They return to familiar phrases like; "We love you baby girl" and "We're so proud of you." Tears flowing, they kiss her forehead and hold each other. There are no blankets to tuck, sheets to straighten, or pillows to fluff. They say, "Goodnight," and express their love one last time before turning away. They have now practiced what it will feel like tomorrow when they will have to turn away the last time, when they will leave her body behind and have their memories and each other to hold.

This time of transition makes her death real; and without it being real, they can't begin to heal. Those who fail to fully embrace the physical, emotional, and relational aspects of death leave themselves insulated in the intellectual knowledge of loss and life. This is where rationalism and realism collide to create something less human and more detached from life and the living. I have always found it oddly inconsistent that the rationalist and realist in the academic communities I've served so often chose to avoid rituals that make death real. Intellectualizing loss is to grieving what imagining being in love is without having a lover: shallow, pointless, detached, and self-centered.

This story is provided to young people who have been ordered to participate in a class called "Crash Course." This course is used to reach the hearts of those who are making choices that have put themselves or others at risk. Jen's story serves as a powerful wake-up call to those who are willing to be open to its messages.

Chapter 7: Gathering

We must engage as many senses as possible…
as soon as possible to begin healing.

As she moves through the room greeting friends, he remains unmoved. His presence is her security and her presence was his meaning. It had been that way since they first met at a dance neither wanted to attend. As we mature we meet our fate . . . or make it. Those who accompany our choices bring their strengths, weaknesses, and choices. These abilities merge to create a possibility beyond the capacity of either alone.

He took her hand and invited her to dance, the spark ignited. Their eyes were fixed on each other's, closing only the brief instance his lips met her cheek as the sunrise peeked through the trees that lined the walk near the side entrance of her dormitory.

They had been alone every day of their lives until that moment . . . thereafter they were never alone again. As she touches the top of his hand and caresses his forearm, her heart aches; he is unmoved.

These hands held hers and placed a ring on her finger that was a symbol of a bond much stronger, brighter, and richer than either could have imagined. These hands fashioned and shaped oak, hickory, pine, and cherry woods until he was their master. He transferred the coarse surface of the wood to his hands and produced furniture, toys, boxes, birdhouses, and homes. Smooth and strong as a young man, she remembers the first time his hands caressed her face and the tingle she still feels with its recollection. These hands bathed their children and washed her back. These hands that held and hugged, carried and coddled, caressed and corrected…now lie cold and still.

They are his hands, yet no longer belong to him. She touches them; they are bumpy and bony now. The gentle brushing against the tiny hair follicles on his hand brings her a moment of slight pleasure; he is unmoved.

She touches his shoulder; the sport jacket she chose is slightly big and the shoulder hidden beneath the shirt feels. . .well it feels bony also. They had not always been this way. She remembers when she'd snuggle under his large arms and pillow-like muscles. She allows herself to drift in her mind to a time they were sleeping nestled together on the hammock in the backyard of their first home.

She combs her fingers through his hair; and remembers the day back in 1966 that he postponed a trip to the barber shop to let his hair grow out. He wasn't going to be a hippie freak, but if it made her happy he'd wear it longer. Soon after, sideburns followed and then wide colorful ties, leisure suits, mustaches, cigars, a fancy car, and the middle years. His hair was wavy . . . she loved that and both enjoyed the attention she gave it.

They laughed together; they cried together; they faced rebellious teens and aging parents . . . together. She counts the times, 1, 2. . .3. Yes, they have been apart only three times in 56 years for a total of seven nights: the hunting trip with the boys, her trip to Las Vegas with the girls, and his trip to New Mexico to plan and attend to his bachelor brother's funeral.

When life has left his body, we realize that he was never just his body. We realize that the "he" we loved was manifested in flesh, but never confined by it. This is how we know our memories are not attached to a body and will live on in the part of us that never dies. We can think this is so, but can't know it until our touch is unfelt by the object of our love.

Those who will not engage the dead physically struggle with this concept because they can only intellectualize their thoughts of love and loss. Physical engagement of the dead is the moment when the spirit made flesh becomes the flesh made spirit. One will never last; the other can never be destroyed.

The viewing of a deceased person is a frequently maligned ritual among many. Perceptions range from fear to disgust, from necessary to useless, from beautiful to barbaric. What is clear is that many value and need this time. What is less obvious is why. Most, if not all, I've ever read on this subject misses three very significant points in caring for the emotional, relational, and spiritual needs of others.

The first is that it is counterintuitive to live one's entire life through the experiences of senses and then expect that simple intellectual assent to the idea of death would be enough for us to begin a healthy grieving process. We are physical beings and grief is a physical experience. We must engage as many senses as possible in the experience, as soon as possible, to begin healing.

The visitation and viewing of the remains hold similar conflict for many families. This leads to my second point. When one becomes a widow or widower, there is a significant social hurdle facing them. That hurdle is being in the presence of friends as a single person again. This transition is best managed while surrounded by family with their deceased loved one still present. In this time, she still belongs to him as he no longer belongs to anyone. His presence comforts her as it pains her. She is not a sad, pathetic, lonely widow who must stoically attend her husband's Memorial Service days or weeks after his death. She is his friend, lover, life changer, playmate, and companion. She is proud their marriage was one of the great ones and that is not ending; she will always be married to this most generous and kind-hearted man. She needs him here, at his own funeral, because she needs him as she faces her new world without him. To face the new world as a widow and to do it without him seems to be a betrayal of that which she has held most dear these many years. How does she move forward without him?

His presence provides her the security necessary in facing a new world, one that won't include him. This enables a widow to see those who are closest to her for the first time while still being a wife, mother, grandmother, and/or sister. It reminds her that, though her primary role has changed, she is still needed, cared for, and loved. She is not presented alone to her friends, as she will be when those who rally to her side for a week or two return to their lives. Not being alone, enjoying the most important achievement of her union, means everything in this moment. As she is surrounded by the handiwork of their lives, she remembers that first kiss and all they shared together.

Finally, as she processes what dead feels like, she begins to imagine what "widow" feels like also. Neither of these is easy or pleasant. She hears people speak for the first time of her husband in the past tense. She then speaks of him the same and it feels odd. It is subtle at first and then profound when phrases like "my husband will," "is," and "can," are replaced by my "husband used to," "was," and "could." She feels what it is like to speak like a widow. These feelings parallel those she had when she wrote her married name the first time; that felt oddly good, this feels the opposite.

Her children tend to her as he once did. He loved to dote on her and look after her every need. As her children hover around, they ask how's she doing, is there anything she needs, can they get her a cup of water, does she need a break. She is grateful to them. They have matured and she is glad that the apple really doesn't fall far from the tree.

Her son arrives late; his plane was delayed. From a distance she sees him take off his coat and talk with the attendant in the hallway. He is the one that reminds her most of the young man she married. His presence brings part of her husband back alive and this thought comforts her. We do live on, if only in parts, within those we love and those who share our DNA. Surrounded by all her children, she sees in each a part of the past and the future. This is what the word legacy must feel like. We all leave one. She likes what the word means to her, and it helps to know that she is part of a bigger story and that just as her ancestors have passed this way, so will she one day.

We gather as family at the time of loss or tragedy because the story of our lives share it's meaning as it is woven within the words, sentences, and chapters of those who know us best. We can play make-believe with anyone, but not with those we grew up with. We can attempt to force others into relationships or out, but those who spent their early years with you know you. Not the carefully constructed, degreed, manicured, faddish caricature of you, but the real you. Sadly, many would rather escape to a self created fantasy than live in a relationship with those who know them best. Requiring a new audience for which to perform, some attempt to create a life where they choose both the audience and applause lines. Their life is predictable and frozen in the safety of their illusions. The death of a loved one can break through those illusions, if only for a moment.

Relationships in families are seldom normal and functional. All families have some level of dysfunction, many are significantly maladjusted. When we gather in these precious but often fragile relationships from our family of origin, we may return to roles and relationships we haven't engaged in for years. The farther removed someone has been from their family, the less likely they are to know how to reenter. This can cause conflict. It is also an opportunity for healing and, for many, the final opportunity to find healing in relationships that last a lifetime.

Death in this environment brings everything into perspective. It makes the profound seem pedestrian, the important seem insignificant, and the petty seem like a complete waste of time and energy.

Transformative life experiences happen because of this reason; and the more fully engaged with the reality of death and the dead we are, the more likely the experience will be transforming. When we neglect the dead, we are at the same time sending a message to the living that they don't matter that much either.

When we fail to allow ourselves to be confronted with the final reality of life, we also fail to provide a context for the significance of love, forgiveness, joy, peace, pleasure, happiness, sadness, and hatred. Hate in the face of death is exposed for the shallow self-centeredness it often is. Love in the face of death exposes our vulnerability to each other and our desperate need for one another. The only thing worse than not forgiving is never forgiving, and death and the dead send this message in **BOLD FONT.**

Gathering is an opportunity for healing the wounds in a family. It also strengthens the healthy bonds that hold us together and which we greatly need in times of loss and mourning.

Chapter 8: Connecting

It's a time for making a connection…the kind of connection that validates a life of complex choices, reassures in time of aloneness and doubt, and gives strength in moments of weakness and tragedy.

Sometimes the best way to understand what is needed is to look at an example that clearly missed the mark. Such was the case with John; he was in his middle 60s and dying of cancer when he contacted me to make his final arrangements. He arrived alone.

John was a gifted and respected academic from a local university who had spent his life teaching and researching in the field of political science. He expressed a desire to "avoid the entanglements of fantasy" in his memorial service. He rejected the notion that his family and friends would need to see his body and believed that religion was a device of the weak-minded to explain things they didn't have the capacity to comprehend.

While I find this attitude devoid of tolerance and sensitivity, my role as a funeral director requires me to understand his perspective, even though it usually comes from someone who had a very bad experience with religion or the religious. In a matter of moments, I discovered that John was a poster child for this view.

I asked if his wife and children felt the same. He stated abruptly, "No, we divorced about 15 years ago when she became a religious nut!" The reason for his hostility to religion had become evident. Unlike most educated people who passionately subscribed to a worldview or philosophy, John was unwilling to take a more reflective view of reality and realize not everyone would or could share his conclusions. John was intensely angry for what he felt religion had done to his life. I must confess this made me wonder if he ever considered that his wife might have felt the same about his academic pursuits.

John had four adult children and nine grandchildren. I explained that remembering his life and the things that were most important to him would help his children and grandchildren participate in a healing ritual. Doing this would add meaning to their experience with his life and death and would help foster healing. Whenever we talk about the things that matter in our lives, whether we are religious or not, we will speak of love, commitment, values, contributions, and relationships. Whether his family's fantasy about ultimate reality included deity or not was not something he would or could control. They would integrate the meaning of his life into the context of their worldview, and he could no more control the outcome of their experience with his death than he could control the cancer that was claiming his life.

A funeral should be an instrument of healing for the living, not a veiled attempt by the dead to settle a score.

I would like to tell you that my advice to John was well received. It was not. As I watched his children and grandchildren listen to his colleagues talk about the great contributions he made to his field of study, I wondered how they felt about his life. No one cried at John's Memorial Service; perhaps it's because they had long ago quit caring. You'd be surprised how often this is the case with the families I serve. The headlong pursuit of self-actualization is often accomplished at the expense of those who need from us something more mundane and less stimulating. John's stubborn refusal to enfold those who saw the world differently didn't start with the planning of his funeral and caused a permanent detachment in life that could not be repaired in death. Ironically, his memorial was then an accurate reflection of his life.

Imagine for a moment what it was like when John's children received the telephone call from his significant other that their father had died the previous evening. They were told the funeral home had already taken him to the crematory and a memorial service was being planned for later in the week.

They were informed by a telephone call that his death occurred 18 hours earlier. He told his girlfriend to tell others to stay away from his deathbed because he didn't want to be seen in such poor condition. More likely, he was avoiding a potentially uncomfortable and messy conflict with his children. Imagine you're his child; to whom will you turn in this moment? How will you begin to cope with the feelings of a relationship that will never be repaired? How do you deal with the loss of a parent you couldn't visit at the end because of his vanity? How do you take the first step to healing when the previous years of living brought pain with no reconciliation?

For many today this is their experience with loss. Unable to restore relationships that are fractured in the present, they are condemned to forever box with the shadows of the past. Finally, denied a moment in the presence of their deceased loved one where they may unburden themselves, they turn to face the future with the unreconciled conflict of the past coloring every relationship they will ever know. Some find healing, most don't and then wonder why life seems so empty and meaningless.

Fortunately, most people are more open to caring for the needs of those they cherish. Connecting with family members at the visitation is a very important part of the healing process. I know from personal experience that a trip to the funeral home is not always the most comfortable experience.

What it feels like to visit . . .

Have you experienced going to a funeral home to visit with someone whose family member has died? Did your heart race a little? Did your palms get sweaty or did you feel a little anxious on the way there? If you experienced any or all of those symptoms, your response is common. As a funeral director, I have those same feelings when I return to the funeral home in my hometown to visit with a childhood friend whose parent has died. I wonder what my friend is like now, especially if I haven't seen them in years. I wonder how they are responding to the death of their parent. I think about my own parents and wonder what it will feel like when I can no longer pick up the telephone and call them. I can remember when his parent was my age and this reminds me of my mortality, and that life doesn't wait for anyone. These thoughts and many others coincide with an ever-elevating blood pressure.

As you enter the funeral home, you feel the awkwardness of not knowing who will be there, which visitation room they will be using, and imagining what the deceased will look like. Hanging your coat, you scan the room for your friend, sign the register book, read the memorial card, scan the room, look for the floral arrangement you sent, and scan the room. You see your friend, he is visiting with others so you find something else to do while you wait in the informal but growing reception line. We don't call it that, but a reception line is what it feels like. You wait your turn to say what you have to say. You keep it brief out of respect for your friend and those waiting behind you. You speak and what you have to say sounds so cliché, "Sorry to hear about your Dad," followed by, "He was a great guy," on the heels of "How is Mom doing?" Then conclude with the mother of all clichés, "Give me a call if there's anything I can do for you." Has anyone either placed or received a call like this? The words feel genuine, the intent is pure, and the likelihood of it ever happening . . . less than 2 percent.

What it feels like to connect . . .

This time, as you enter the visitation room it feels different. As you wait to talk with your friend, you watch people visiting and many are laughing. They are holding pictures, looking at golf clubs, fishing poles, and a Harley Davidson that was positioned to the left of the casket. You look at the front of the memorial card and see a picture of your friend's dad. However, it isn't like the hundreds of others you've seen. This is more like a photo and it makes you smile. It's a picture of the deceased doing what he loved to do in life; he was riding his Harley into the evening sunset.

Visitation at the funeral home is a time for making a connection, a simple human connection - the kind of connection that validates a life of complex choices, reassures in time of aloneness and doubt, and gives strength in moments of weakness and tragedy. Human connection, both expressive and silent, is our security amidst the storms of life. We search for this kind of connection in many ways through the course of our lives. The spectrum of these connections leads us to enjoy getting to know a friend at a deeper, more real level or avoid relational entanglements we believe will be unhealthy, unsafe, or even unkind.

When we host events that mark the important milestones of life, we invite others to join us. Graduations, baby-showers, retirement parties, and marriage ceremonies are often measurements of the connections we have with others. Though these events may measure the breadth of our relationships and attachments to others, they do not tell us much of the depth. I have been surprised to be in the wedding parties of virtual strangers, and surprised to not be invited to events I thought for certain I would. Funerals are not this way. When our loved ones die, those who come to see us choose to; and this is based on their perception of the depth of attachment to the deceased or family members.

Former New York City Mayor Rudy Giuliani once said that for a leader in any organization, weddings were optional, funerals were mandatory. To convey our willingness to be with someone in the darkest hours of their lives says, without the use of words, they are loved and their loss matters.

It is common for the media, political parties, and the public to "celebrate" the contributions of our national leaders at the time of their deaths. The death of President Ronald Reagan is a prime example. Millions upon millions mourned his death. The man they knew had been a living symbol of the nation, a useful and skilled political leader, and perhaps the greatest communicator (connector) to ever hold the office of President. Yet, in biography after biography we find that he was aloof to those closest to him. It seems he was a man who could connect with and lead millions of people, but struggled to connect with his children and grandchildren.

What is missing is human connection at the most fundamental level. The ability to forge a deep connection is the one thing above and beyond all others that allows us to begin healing when we lose someone we knew and to whom we were deeply attached. In the earlier story John refused this opportunity for his children and grandchildren. Even without a formal religious ceremony, they would have benefited from being with those who respected their father and hearing stories and accepting their expression of sorrow. Memorial services do not provide the time necessary for this kind of human connection; most people show up 15 minutes before the ceremony and leave shortly thereafter. It is the perfect ceremony for those wishing to keep their feelings private and others at a distance.

Superficial relationships of convenience or expedience are

exposed in times of tragedy. When people die, those who are now charged with the task of grieving begin to look to others to frame and understand the meaning and significance of their loved one's life. Many times the qualities they most cherished were enjoyed by others as well. This recognition brings comfort and validation to their grieving, while confirming their personal choice to share their life with the deceased. It comforts them to know the qualities they admired and loved were appreciated by others, like the way a parent finds joy in watching their child become excited by an activity, sport, task, or hobby that they had loved as a child. Sharing part of our loved one with others brings shared joy and this comforts the grieving.

All humans, even the elderly, seek validation of their choices and talents. When we recall to the grieving a story that honors their mate, we are at the same time validating their choice of mate, their commitment to lifelong love, and the worthiness of their shared sacrifices and challenges.

Everyone's life is a story, a narrative of personal meaning, an unfolding of themes and characters that come in and out of our lives, each adding to the story of our lives as we add to the story of theirs. When we die, our stories, themes, and character come to an end. The meaning of each of these will be shaped by those who survive. Though our story ends when we die, it lives on in the lives of those who survive us; and those lives will be changed permanently thereafter. John's story was an autobiography; not surprisingly, his service concluded with Frank Sinatra's famous narcissistic rendition of "I Did It My Way."

The dead will be remembered as a character in the story of their family. Survivors are left to ponder both how the deceased contributed to the larger story of their family and friends, and how they shaped the lives of those closest to them. How did they change the nature of their family's narrative? What is their legacy within their family?

When we visit with the grieving, we connect because we have shared part of the journey with someone we both cared for. When this is not the case, when we didn't know their loved one, we invite ourselves into what will be a difficult chapter in their lives. This is why most small communities and ethnic groups have commonly accepted rituals at the time of loss that include their community. They shared their lives: good and bad, work and play, prosperity and scarcity, and fought with and against each other. They could no more exclude their community at the time of loss or tragedy than they could or would their family. Transients seldom experience this, and their life stories are focused on personal satisfaction or indulgence and communal detachment.

This is why some in our culture choose little if any ritual at the time of death. Little connection is required because little connection was ever made with the outside world. Requiring or giving little to anyone in life won't change at death. If I've learned one thing in watching the grieving over 25 years, it is that dysfunctional people tend to be even more so when confronted with something as disquieting to the psyche or soul as the death of a loved one.

Those who are selfish, angry, bitter, vindictive, self righteous, indulgent, and reclusive, tend to become more so when facing the death of a loved one. Conversely, the emotionally and relationally healthy tend to express their grief in ways that are healthy for themselves and their loved ones.

This is not surprising and shouldn't be. Psychosocial dynamics and developmental tasks evolve across the span of life. For those who have become foreclosed in their development, something as traumatic as the death of a loved one can open wounds and neuroses that have been buried for decades. This explains why, in the first days of loss, the emotionally underdeveloped retreat to familiar, unhealthy, defensive mechanisms and methods of managing this pain. The death of a loved one can offer a time for life transformation or regression. One thing is for certain, it will not leave us unchanged.

Those who have deep roots in their community must include them in their healing process. Connection with others sustains us in the most difficult times and provides the healthy context for shared suffering that enables deep relationships, bonds, and attachments to become even deeper. Those who walk with us in the dark hour will be those who will celebrate the real joys of life.

Sharing the depth of loss and soulful grief provides the context for the good things in life to be better, the inconsequential experiences in life to be meaningful, the subtle events of life to be made significant, and the simplest expression of love or generosity to be profound.

To gain acceptance we must risk rejection. To gain intimacy with others we must risk conflict. To know love we must risk suffering. To be fully known by others we must risk humiliation. It is the only path available to reach a vital engagement with others and life. The only other choice is to withdraw to a place of measured risk that leads to shallow relationships and social detachment. Many forsake the depth of love, intimacy, acceptance, and full engagement with another human being for false engagements. They judge individual worth by material acquisitions; professional value by degrees, titles, and achievements; enlightenment by subjective narcissistic worldviews; and esteem by the opinion of those who don't know themselves any better than they know us.

Death confronts the emptiness of this façade and declares with a deafening persistence, "Is that all there is?" and, "Is this the sum total of life's pursuits?" Death will shred façades and illusions, if only for a moment, and provide us with a life check. This is the underlying reason many shun the practice of viewing the dead and shun rituals around death. Mining through the messages sent by the dead, both subconscious and conscious, is too intimidating. Tragically, we then miss one of life's greatest opportunities to understand more deeply what life is really all about.

With each death the willingness to be open to these life lessons is expanded or diminished, and with it the opportunities to more fully engage or detach from the things that matter most in life. It is not possible to fully embrace love, intimacy, joy, and deep human connection without confronting the awfulness of what dead looks like.

The dead remind us that we are not the sum of our goods, resources, or accolades. The dead remind us we are worm food: the rich and poor, the educated and uneducated, the kind and cruel. The dead remind us there is a foe or force that we all confront and that no one beats. Death is the level setter of all humanity.

This is what those closest to a death know at some level. Our pulse races, palms get sweaty, and blood pressure elevates because we are exposing ourselves to the hurt of others and the possibility that the existence to which we have given ourselves might be exposed as trite. This lurks beneath the surface of everyone close to a death as we wonder who will gather to remember us when we've been reduced to dust or we're lying in the casket.

Connecting with those who have shared life and love with us, forces us to begin to reflect on the meaning of life and how we live our lives. Life-transforming experiences are directly associated with how much time one is willing to spend reflecting on the life of the deceased and considering the choices and habits of our lives. For many this process is new and intimidating. Many quickly abandon this opportunity for personal growth and return to the unexamined life they had before the death occurred.

Foreclosing on grief will lead to the same with almost every area of life. Most will remain that way until the next life tragedy comes along. Many choose to medicate, both legally and illegally, on substances and habits that numb the pain of their loss and foster the abandonment of a richer, deeper life. Unfortunately, the consequence of this choice is to be the empty shell of the person they could have been.

Chapter 9: Reflecting

A eulogy I was too young to give…

Most of us have someone in our lives we'd like to say thank you to for the way they influenced our lives. At times we don't realize their influence for many years. Reflecting in this way is similar to what we do when someone we loved has died. We think about how they influenced us, gave of themselves, and overcame challenges. Reflective thinking in this way adds depth to our memories and insights. One person I remember fondly, and was too young to tell him personally, was Richard Sullens.

Mr. Sullens was my Little League baseball coach. He coached the Astros and he led us to two division championships and one league championship.

Mr. Sullens was not the rah-rah kind of coach. He didn't seek to make you afraid of him or to be your friend. He was a coach, plain and simple. Long before organizations talked about the value of shared ethos and culture, Mr. Sullens played things straight; you knew where you stood and what he expected from you. We were children being respected as ballplayers, and this made us feel important on the outside and very good on the inside. He inspired loyalty that made us never want to disappoint him. He did this by doing things the right way, for the right reason, and treated his most and least talented players the same way.

Coaching at this level can be among the most difficult. Most parents think their child is better than he is and blame the coach for not figuring that out. Mr. Sullens put me at first base the very first practice and I never played elsewhere. The more he told me I could, the more I wanted to and did; to this day I don't know which comes first, encouragement or talent. As a coach I don't wait for talent to surface, I name it, call it out, and keep reminding the fledgling of their potential; when I do this I remember Mr. Sullens.

The morals and ethics I was raised with were manifested with Mr. Sullens' Astros. If you win, don't think yourself too good and if you lose, always honor your opponent's victory. The practice of sportsmanship is like any cherished characteristic or moral - it only matters when it's hard. We were told to do it and, mostly, we did. Failure on the playing field seldom brought reproach; failure to have a good competitive attitude could buy you some time on the bench.

Mr. Sullens would tell us that we would get lucky if we worked hard. His life seemed to be a direct reflection of this truth. He did work hard, very hard. He had a loving and lovely wife, active boys, and seemed to manage it all without breaking a sweat. Our games felt like practice because his verbal encouragement was the same. They included, but were by no means limited to, phrases like, "stay alert", "just focus on the pitch being thrown", "cheer for your teammates", "cover your position", "back-up those next to you", "hold the runners", "never give up an easy run", and "make your opponent work for everything".

The day I heard he was diagnosed with a brain tumor I wept. The day he died I bawled. He was in his 50s. That was old to me then and young to me now.

The news of his death was even more poignant because his son Bruce, the catcher on our team, was only a year younger than I was. You're aware from a young age that your parents will die. When it happens the first time to a friend's father, you look at your own differently from that day forward.

This sturdy strong man, who could throw an underhand fast pitch past me anytime he wanted three years earlier, eventually struggled to walk and then to breathe. He fought and struggled I'm told, until death proved stronger. Hard work hadn't produced the expected luck this time.

Among presidents and politicians much is made of the word legacy… this is a desire at some level to be of consequence in human history. Mr. Sullens was someone who validated what my parents had taught me with the doing of it. The doing of it is what gives others the courage to do it also. Some talk: others have high ideas, but remain locked in an inactive silence. Mr. Sullens showed up, did his best, encouraged others to do the same, and as such remains an inspiration these many years later.

I don't remember what he looked like in his casket. I've tried to recall and can't. I can recall what he looked like standing in our dugout, pitching batting practice, hitting grounders during infield practice, and smiling.

I remember seeing his sons and feeling very sad. I remember seeing Mrs. Sullens and wanting her to know that I shared a small portion of the affection she had for her husband. Both memories can bring tears if I think about it for too long.

Had Mr. Sullens died an elderly man, news of his death would have caused similar reflections but the heaviness of the loss would not have been the same. When he died, his family, children, and grandchildren lost many years of fun and love. When one dies young, the mourners cling to the memories of the past and are left with the pain of future losses. Initially, life events for everyone in the family are affected as the absence of the deceased is prominent in the minds of those present. We wonder aloud how much they are missed, how much they would enjoy being there, we anticipate how they would feel and what they would do.

I never had a chance to say thank you to Mr. Sullens. For many years this bothered me. Having now coached baseball for my children, I recognize the thanks are found in the doing. It is the little things we do in life that can be monumental. I was just one of perhaps a hundred boys he coached; having talked with some of them, I realize they share both the great memories and the loss I feel, this comforts me.

When we find meaning in our shared loss, we are comforted because we know we are not alone. There is a sense of knowing what is shared without speaking, a sense of loss without counting, and a sense of belonging that reaches the deepest parts of our soul. As loss weakens our spirit, reflecting on the good strengthens us as we determine to become what we long for, to create what has been lost, and to pass on the best of what we've been given.

To do this one must take time to reflect on those things that the deceased did that inspired and enlarged our world. The only path to this enlightenment is the painful journey of reflecting on our losses. Losses are actually gifts in disguise that will be with us forever. They feel like losses because the gift giver is no longer with us. Remember, a gift from the heart and soul can never be lost; it is to be valued and passed on. It is only when we reflect deeply on what was shared that we can fully appreciate what was lost, and acting on these gifts is the essential basis of beginning to heal.

The habit of reflective thinking is familiar to some and completely alien to others. This habit doesn't appear to be associated with IQ. I've known the simple to be profound and the complex to be clueless when wrestling with the issues of life and death. When we experience loss, we will find ourselves thinking about our loved one - their life, the life we shared with them - and trying to figure out what it all means. I have heard some describe being lost in their thoughts for hours in the days and weeks after loss.

Reflective thinking is a habit that can help those dealing with tragedy. This leads us to this very important question; how do we begin healing? Is there an indicator, a moment when we can know that we have begun the journey out of the valley of the shadow of death? This moment occurs when we realize the thing we thought we lost was actually a gift that must be given to others in order to begin our healing.

This is when the introspective moments of reflection and revelation are manifested in the conscious choice to become a gift giver. This is how our loved ones live on, and the impact and influence of their lives can both foster healing within us and add meaning to our lives and to others in the present.

The saddest widows and widowers I meet are the ones who have spent years exhausting the tragedy of their losses, never converting them to a blessing for others. I suspect this mirrors the nature of the person. If they lived as primary beneficiary of their lost love's life, like a sponge that is never saturated, then it is likely they will be more focused on what they've lost than how they can use what they've been given. The psychological term for finding the good within the bad is sublimation. Sublimation is the skill or ability to extract the best from the difficult or tragic events of life. Almost everyone has a Mr. Sullens in their past. Taking time to reflect on their lives can be a valuable exercise, which can enhance our present relationships as we learn to move from gift receiver to gift giver.

Reflecting on the life of our deceased friend or family member, and carefully inventorying their impact and influence in our lives, is the catalyst for embracing the meaning of their life and significance of their death. It is as we celebrate, as we experience joy that something good or special has come from our loss, that we begin to heal.

Inventorying our gifts may make us miss the gift giver; it will also allow them to be alive in us as we share those gifts with others.

These are the two faces of a healthy grieving experience: sadness and joy, celebration and grief, aching for more and grateful for what we had. Embracing both can only occur through reflective thinking on the meaning and value of each of them.

Lopsided acute loss management leaves one off balance emotionally, relationally and spiritually. Some try, from the earliest moments of loss, to put on a happy face and think happy thoughts in an attempt to push away the negative. This can lead to a life that seems ever more dull, listless, and joyless. Others put on a sad face, constantly ruminating on what was lost, fearing what comes next, effectively taking up residence in sorrow and the land of psycho pharmaceuticals. Sadness and joy have their place in loss; and providing a time and place for both can help the grieving to return to life - as different as it may be - that can be as, or more, satisfying than before.

I have witnessed thousands attempt to traverse this journey. While there is no perfect way to travel, there are only two ending points; they are wholeness or brokenness. The decision you make in the immediate days following the death of a loved one will place you on track to arrive at one or the other. This is where funeral directors can join the healing profession, by helping their clients to begin healing. Failure to do so is to provide a meaningless ritual at a needless expense.

Chapter 10: Celebrating

Measuring the fullness of life in the face of death and the things that matter most…

Being asked to host a Celebration of Life is an event that is hard to decline. Two of the three words in this phrase are uplifting. There have not been too many lives that were not worth celebrating. All lives have made an impact on someone. Each person has influence on those around him or her. A Celebration of Life should focus on the things that matter the most to the person who has died and to the family who is surviving. By acknowledging the things that matter most to us we are beginning to inventory our losses, attempting to define their meaning, embracing what was given to us, and preparing to be a giver of the same to others. These tasks are at the heart of what it means to celebrate and why setting this in motion for a grieving family is the catalyst for embracing their loss and to begin healing.

Just the word "celebrating" makes us feel better. The word "funeral" doesn't have the same effect. Oddly, both serve the exact same purpose and functions. The word "funeral," for many, draws up memories and images of dreaded or awful experiences. When most people think of the word, they envision a dimly lit room decorated with nice but slightly dated furniture with an odd flowery smell that shields people dressed in mourning black, who are alternately hugging and crying. Dead resides in a box that has a corpse half hidden from view. The heavy décor masks and absorbs the excruciating feelings of acute loss that many in our culture seem to believe we weren't supposed to see or feel.

Dead, even half-hidden, stuns even the most stoic among us, because it's hard to touch a cold lifeless body without acknowledging that we will one day become bloodless and breathless. At the moment we see dead, it reminds us that it will come get us one day. We are scared with a deep inner repulsiveness that strikes the core of our being and is unlike any other feeling we have as humans. As mortals, we are facing our mortality. As recipients of human existence, the religious and unreligious prefer to think of life as a miracle. Funeral means all of the above for many, and for all the end of their miracle. Funerals are seen as the biggest yuck of life.

Most have heard the term a Celebration of Life to describe the type of memorial or funeral service a family would like to have for the deceased. This phrase became more popular for those who chose to cremate their loved ones. The intention is noble, but sadly meaningless when taken out of context and the presence of the dead. Just as the word "good" has no meaning without the word "evil," celebrating life without a symbol of death causes the terms themselves to be shallow in meaning. Life and the celebration thereof have little meaning or context when celebrated at places and among people where the dead are unwelcome. Imagine "yin" without "yang" or "milk" without "shake." This may seem simplistic; but when we engage our minds in Celebrating, we must also engage our hearts in embracing what has been lost. These are the two faces of loss that will accompany the grieving throughout their experience.

Marketers have a habit of changing words to make their products more acceptable to their clients. It is why we call it life insurance when we buy a policy to protect our family at the time of our death. It is interesting that the phrase, A Celebration of Life, originated with funeral consumers. The phrase came into fashion about 25 years ago and is used by most funeral homes today, usually when a family requests it.

Words have meaning, and for the family of a 12-year-old-boy who died unexpectedly, the words used meant the difference between having an experience that helped them heal and one that would haunt them for years to come. His father, Jim, stated clearly, "I can't have a funeral for my son, but I can Celebrate His Life!" Four days later, as we released a dove at the grave of his son, he whispered to his wife, "Our little boy was such a gift, I'm so glad God gave him to us." His next words pointed forward, "We're going to make it, Honey . . . We're going to make it."

We cannot deeply celebrate life without profoundly grieving. These dramatic swings in emotion are an indicator of the depth of our awareness of what has been lost. Later, they serve as measuring devices that help us consciously recognize the loss and emerge from grief. Failure to provide time, place, and context for both leaves the grieving with faulty measuring devices and an emotional wound that can dull the joys, happiness, and meaning of every relationship and each life event. The physical presence of the dead makes all the difference in fully experiencing what has been lost. Imagine your child giving birth and the only connection with the child is the telephone call you receive afterwards. How real would your connection be with the grandchild? The difference between word and flesh is profound.

Most Celebration of Life services I've seen are awkward attempts of putting a happy face on the most devastating of human experiences. These services are usually filled with platitudes, and the depth of real emotion expressed is equal to the time those closest to the death actually spent in the presence of the dead. Like a stone skipping across the water, when we lose the energy that propels us above the surface, we will plunge into a depth of sadness only those who have honestly faced loss can know.

The dead don't lie to us about their condition. They don't say they are doing fine, they can't run from what has happened, and they can't mask their true feelings. It seems the dead don't move, but can easily move us to tears. They will never again raise an eyebrow of curiosity, show a frown of disgust, or shed a tear of joy. Though we saw them a hundred times when they were living and never cried, now in their presence we can't stop. This fact must make us ask "Why?" It should also make us ask why some would choose to avoid this most final of all realities. Why do we cry by simply seeing the dead but don't when seeing them alive? At times of great joy or reunions, people who have been separated by time or tragedy cry in the presence of each other.

Many cry when seeing a friend, hearing a song, and/or seeing a movie that reminds them of the deceased. We cry because they shared their life with us and added to ours in the process. We cry because they cared for and loved us, as we loved them. We cry, because we are faced with the ultimate measuring device of life. We are reminded that nothing is permanent, that all things shall pass; and even as we look to the security of those who are still with us, we imagine one day they will grieve us or we will grieve them.

Some push the feelings of loss deep beneath their superficial appearance and in a pseudo-courageous act determined to express only one dimension of their loss and limit others to the same. It's as if they say, "I just ripped from my being the one I named the flesh of my flesh 52 years ago; now let's go throw a party. Let's have a beer, roast a pig, and gather at the Club. I will not succumb to the awfulness of this moment. I will rise above, devoted to the goodness of life and the greatest of my loved one." The emotional crash that follows these kinds of events will be experienced in isolation and will not be celebrated. If grief is forever postponed, then life and love will be diminished everyday thereafter. We can't love beyond our ability to grieve.

Chapter 11: Gift Receiver to Gift Giver

Within our broken hearts we will find the source of our healing and become a gift giver, life giver!

The fact that most people have a deep aversion to the topic of death and a great fear of their own death is nothing new. This aversion and fear is unlike anything we experience in life because everything else pales in comparison. Unfortunately, being fearful complicates our feelings and thoughts, as lightning intensifies an ordinary rainstorm. Rain, while unwelcome, generally doesn't make us feel threatened; add the element of lightning and the potential for personal harm makes the need to seek shelter essential. Similarly, the news that someone we know has died isn't as threatening as hearing the news that we have a terminal illness. For most of our lives we are able to keep the thoughts of death at a distance by escaping into the busyness of life or our chosen vocations.

When death visits we face both a trauma and a choice. We can use this confrontation with ultimate reality to expand the possibilities of life and love or collapse inward to focus on only the "self." Will we become more or less? We will not be left the same!

For those who make room for their feelings of loss and attempt to name specifically what they miss or grieve, the weight of loss can seem almost unbearable. Each reflection of the good is accompanied by the aching of our hearts and recognition of yet another good memory turned painful. The first year can feel this way and, for many, the second year is almost worse.

This is an emotionally trying process; the benefits of embracing what was lost will come. Time doesn't heal all wounds; time allows us the opportunity to put them in perspective and then choose what to do with what we've been given.

Loss is made meaningful when it affirms life.

Denial of, or suppression of, the feelings of loss disavows and disinherits life. Tragically, faced with the choice of mining through the cavernous feeling of loss, many return to the routine of an unanalyzed life.

Modern life is measured by many devices. Among them are net worth, notoriety, celebrity, college degrees, sexual conquests, political movements, and spiritual quests. These provide a way to quantify the value of our lives. Experiencing some success leads many to seek to "super size" their knowledge, quest, or gift in an attempt to authenticate their journey, to gain the acceptance and applause of others, and to prove their uniqueness among the masses. YouTube, Twitter, Facebook and other online services exploit the common person's desire/need for super sizing and validating their life experience. When death interrupts, most will attempt to quickly return to the routine of life and use their favorite form of escapism to drown out the turmoil inside their heads that is magnified during times of loss.

Time passes, others we know die. We look in the mirror and see in our reflection wrinkles forming, and with them emerges a message of nagging self-doubt that declares something is amiss and we do not know what it is. We think this is foolish, and that descending into the land of the lost, depressed souls isn't going to achieve anything.

We don't say these things out loud, but most think that time given to grief and sadness is essentially time wasted. We put a brave face on grief and draw up phrases like "carpe diem" to propel us back into a lie of sameness and safety. Then, in the quiet hour of life, in the moments before we fall asleep, we hear a voice that asks, "Is this all there is? Is something missing?" In this quiet the voice compels us to listen, promising a painful journey, with an unknown timetable that leads to a life of vitality and richness. We all hear this voice. Perhaps the questions are different, and if we tune the voices out, they will eventually leave. For the student who is unwilling to learn, or is simply unready, the teacher lies dormant until the next death or tragedy.

What is amiss? For many it is the ability to reflect about one's life. In this book, I've tried to help you begin a journey of reflective thinking, as you read about death and life through the eyes of the grieving. The voice inside you that asks reflective questions about the purpose of one's life, the ability to be true to one's self, the willingness to change, the courage to reinvent, the initiative to tackle new challenges, and the charity to reengage broken relationships will seldom emerge from the routine of life. It occurs when the dead speak to us and ask questions that can haunt us until we seek the answers.

Good answers to these questions tend to lead us to even better, more personal questions that are tailored to the specific needs in our lives. The more we seek, the deeper, the more enriching our lives become. Initially, the questions vary from superficial questions like "Am I happy?" to extremely painful questions such as "Can I ever be happy again?" More questions may follow:

- For those stuck in a life that feels out of control, they may consider if they are living life by intention or accident?

- For some, rethinking unhealthy life habits may lead them to review the impact of their choices and how they were influenced by their family of origin?
- The person who feels they have underachieved in life may ask if they are capable of more**?**
- Someone who seeks a deeper understanding of life may ask if there is an ultimate and absolute purpose in life?
- A repressed contemplative may consider for the first time the meaning of the things that matter to them and ask the question of the meaning of life?
- The one who has accomplished much but still feels empty inside may ask what makes their life significant?
- The religiously underdeveloped or previously disinterested may seek new answers to their questions about God.
- The lonely or lonesome may ask if anyone really cares?
- The hopeless may wonder if they will always feel that way.
- The addict may confront their addiction.
- A person that has nagging questions about their ability to succeed may ask if they will ever live up to their potential?
- The elderly may ask if they have done all they could with what they've been given?

These are just some of the questions you may hear in the quiet hour; there are many, many more. To these questions about life, death warns us to start acting on them now because life is not a dress rehearsal. These questions may cause us to reconsider our view of the world and our life choices. Our answers are limited to the ability to reflectively consider and then imagine another path.

Patience for the petty or trivial will be more limited as reflecting on the things that really matter begins to take precedent. Perhaps we need to ask different questions, seek a different kind of knowledge, redefine what it means to be human, and cast off the limits of routine and commonly accepted constraints. Instead of pursuing the means that exploit our senses, perhaps we should embrace those things that enhance and expand our potential.

Those who are unwilling to delve into this journey will seek to suppress uncomfortable feelings and disorienting questions or doubts. Many will return to whatever form of escape they used prior to their loss. Some will choose the pursuit of pleasure, entertainment, academia, psychotherapy, sexuality, political activism, business ventures, and religious constructs to define and measure their value and purpose in life. While any one of these may have a fruitful purpose, each can serve as an unhealthy escape from thoughts of mortality and serve to limit human growth.

In over 25 years as a funeral director, I have witnessed thousands of healthy families attempting to grieve a loss. I have had the privilege of watching the elderly widow or widower grieve the loss of their friend, love, playmate, and companion who honored their commitment to grow old together, for better or worse, richer or poorer, and in sickness and health, until death separated them. If you listen to what the widow or widower talks about, you will learn that life was and is measured by what they were able to overcome, share, and celebrate. What becomes obvious in observing these couples is that the commitment to lifelong love has provided the security necessary to empower their family with the ability to find the good in the struggles and challenges of life.

I have also observed many dysfunctional families, such as in the case of a deceased man who had left his wife for another woman, leading to the meeting that took place with the new wife and the man's children. The children viewed the new wife as having killed their family and, while dealing with the death of their father, relived that death too. The discomfort felt by the new wife was also obvious.

There are the empty stares and inability of one sibling to empathize with the needs of another because they were torn apart 40 years ago by parents who were more worried about pursuing their own fulfillment than caring for their children. Or the 73-year-old woman, who while giving a eulogy, spoke of being raped by the man we were burying that day. Or the daughter who screamed "You M***** F****** B****" as she stood over her mother's casket.

Perhaps, if these voices had been heard earlier they might have caused a time of reflection that could have led to forgiveness and healing. Maybe it would have led the elderly woman to seek counseling about the rape. It may have been a way for the mother and daughter to come to terms with their pasts and develop a loving relationship.

Every person has the ability to grow, and reflection is the starting point. Developing and investing in oneself enables you to contribute meaningfully to the lives of others. This rationale flies in the face of most modern thought, which leads people to believe that they can find happiness in self-centered and self-serving pursuits. Happiness will remain elusive until one decides how to best contribute to the well-being of others. Takers never get enough of what they need; givers always have more than enough to give away. This is true even if both start with exactly the same portions of gifts. One seeks happiness in their pursuit; the other uses their pursuit to help others.

When death interrupts the natural routine of our pursuits, it asks us to reflect on the things that matter the most. These things are seldom profound or scintillating. They are not usually accompanied by a degree or award. Avoidance of death rituals and the dead is a form of denial and reflects an unwillingness to confront the reality of life as we live it.

When allowed to do its work, reflective thinking about one's life at the time of death will either reinforce or confront our existing choices. How will you know which to expect? That answer is relatively simple. Are you still taking from life, like a junkie who needs his fix, or are you giving to life? In the end, death will teach you that your life didn't belong to you, but to anyone who ever cared about you. Life in its purest and richest form will be willing to risk all to give all not to gain it. The ancient scripture proclaims, "What does it profit a man who gains the whole, world but loses his soul?" Humanity will consume itself when the takers outnumber the givers.

In the end we do not fear dying, we fear living. We fear that we might not get what we need and, therefore, horde much more than we will ever use. Of the many ways people can be divided or categorized today, perhaps there are two words that describe the basic nature in all of us; we are either takers or givers. If we fear being hurt by takers, we surrender the best that life has to offer. Takers are simply people who are trying to fill the void created by the narrow expression of their pursuit of happiness. Takers live marginal lives. Exploiting one component of what it means to be human and neglecting the rest. At funerals, no one ever talks about what someone took from this world, only what they gave to it. As such, takers have short funerals or avoid the process altogether.

The ultimate task of human development is to move from gift receiver to gift giver. As we examine our lives and losses, we can know we've begun the process of healing when we identify ourselves as giving to another a gift we have been given by the one who has died. We can only do this by inventorying all that was lost because of their death and accounting for all that was given to us during their life. Out of our sadness we will find those things that bring joy to others and ourselves. Within our broken hearts we will find the source of our healing and the ability to become a gift giver and life giver.

Chapter 12: Beyond the Choice of Burial or Cremation

A new narrative with an old purpose

To all who read this book, I would invite you to look beyond the question of burial or cremation. As a professional funeral director, I will tell you that the final disposition of your loved one's body is a personal decision and the least consequential choice you will make when planning a loss experience. The choices of how you will attend to the emotional, relational, and spiritual needs of your family are far more important questions and the ones I've attempted to address in this book.

This book is not an attempt to refute the claims of funeral industry critics. If anyone in any business is exploitive or manipulative, I would hope that others, self-appointed or otherwise, would shine light on their transgressions. My intention is to assert that there are essential tasks in the human experience of loss that are best addressed in the first 10 days. This is a new narrative with an old purpose. Funeral directors have the experience; and if they choose to become experts on how to nurture these essential tasks, they will earn the moral authority to serve and the professional respect most seek.

Smoke and Fire

It has been said that where there is smoke, there is fire. For more than 40 years the media, academic and social elites, and industry critics have fanned the flames of accusations that the funeral business as a whole, and funeral directors specifically, are exploitive of the vulnerable and that the funeral process is excessive, gaudy, barbaric, and needless. They originally promoted cremation and now encourage cremation, green funerals, and do-it-yourself celebrations as the alternative to "being taken advantage of by your local funeral home." For much of my early career I listened to these accusations, tried to understand the accusers' alarm, and often felt a kindred spirit with many in regard to their concerns.

As a newcomer to the funeral business, with no family ties or previous employment history, I approached my education at Mortuary School as a skeptic. I admit that some of what I learned at school about how to operate a funeral business was troubling. Because of the nature of this transaction, most people are ill-prepared to make the decisions they must. This provides the opportunity for abuse or manipulation that our critics declare is universal.

While abuses can still occur, government regulation has provided an unsuspecting consumer with a decent measure of protection. What regulation cannot achieve is often addressed by competition and normal market forces, which continue to have a positive impact on behalf of consumers.

Beyond the practices that I found troubling was a much more perplexing and disquieting concern for the long-term welfare of funeral service and the families we serve. This concern is directed at the lack of a universal or unifying vision for what a funeral director should do for the living. Put differently, if we as a culture continue to hire people to assist us in disposing of the remains of our loved ones, shouldn't they possess the skills, abilities, and professional capacity to provide a therapeutic, interactive, and empowering experience for those who survive? Tragically, nurturing this kind of experience, even to this day, is almost completely ignored at most Mortuary Schools. Yet nothing is more critical to the long-term potential of a future funeral director and the profession he or she will serve.

After 40 years of challenges and reacting to outside pressures, the funeral industry still doesn't know how to answer the simplest of questions about what they do for ***the*** living. Their understanding of what consumers need from them is practically non-existent. Most have an intuitive feel for the value of what they see happening for the families they serve, but do not have the language or constructs to communicate this to their client. Therefore, the profession has no coherent or universal vision for how to best serve those in need.

If you doubt this is true, pick up your local phonebook and call five funeral homes. Ask to speak with the manager or director, and pose this question: Why should I choose your funeral home? The manager or director will tell you about who they are, how long they have been in business, talk about the size of their building or parking lot, and mix in words like *compassionate, kind,* and *integrity.* If they answer this way, they are telling you they don't know why you should choose their funeral home. If they don't know why you should choose their funeral home, they don't know what business they are in. If they don't know what business they are in, they will not have an intentional plan to help you and your family. To receive the greatest value for the money you will spend, the funeral home you choose must have a plan to help your family begin healing *regardless* if you choose cremation or burial.

Some funeral directors may tell you that "a funeral is for the living." If that's all the advice they have to offer, with no intentional plan to help ***the*** living, this expression comes across more like "a funeral helps me make a living." If they tell you that funerals are for *the* living, ask them what they do to help *the* living. Insist on specifics. Expect something more than an impressive entrance, nicely decorated rooms, comfy furniture, clean bathrooms, a large parking lot, and the willingness to be kind to you at one of the most difficult times in your life.

Most funeral directors will take information from you to determine how, where, and when they will dispose of your loved one's body. They'll be nice to you, empathetic and genuine, but they'll never address the question of "why" you made a specific choice. The answer to "Why?" has to do with the needs of your family. All the other questions revolve around what they will do for the deceased. As fewer and fewer people choose rituals to assist their family's loss experience, one might think the funeral industry would be motivated to find answers to the significant "why" question.

Instead, some have expanded their disposition business to include kindly caring for the disposition of the family cat and dog. This allows them to stay in their comfort zone of the "how," "where," and "when" questions. Others have begun to offer luncheons and reception facilities, because they understand the need for food and can ask questions about what and how many. If they understood the therapeutic value of meaningful ritual in caring for your emotional, relational, and spiritual needs, perhaps they wouldn't have to bury *Fluffy* or become caterers. These are vain attempts to find a magic bullet that will temporarily rescue their economic status. Don't mistake these for services that will help your family begin healing.

Critics of this process need to understand that those who choose ritual at the time of loss are ever more aware and educated consumers. They choose ritual because they need ritual. Many families who followed media warnings in the past and chose direct cremation during their last death experience now choose ritual before cremation. They may not know why; they simply know that the previous choice was shallow, empty, and afterwards complicated their grief experience.

What is clear to me is that most families recognize that ritual at the time of loss helps them through the loss experience. My experience in observing families these many years is that most people need a time, place, and someone to coach them through the experience of loss. Those who do provide a ritual that contains the seven phases mentioned in this book will nurture a healthy grieving experience for themselves and others.

Why some families do or don't choose a meaningful ritual at the time of loss has been a source of constant personal study and observation for me over the past three decades. What is clear is that those who do not choose a meaningful ritual will often delay, and sometimes forever foreclose on, a healthy experience with grief.

My observations have led me to conclude that there are several psycho-social behaviors and trends that have emerged, and in many cases combined in the past 40 years that impact consumer choices. It is my belief that these behaviors and trends are equal to if not more significant in, shaping our clients' choices, than the desire among some to avoid funeral expenses. These behaviors and trends include, but are not limited to, the influence of negative media, the escalating divorce rate, fractured families, dysfunctional families, a growing transient populace, and the influence of elite communities on popular culture.

Influence of Negative Media

First, the influence of negative media tends to be, for most of our clients, subconscious. In almost 30 years of dealing with families, I've never had one mention that their choice in disposition was directly affected by a specific news story they had watched. Though not remembering a specific report, they tend to hold general concepts and the common message which is to "avoid getting ripped off by funeral homes." This results in a small but growing number of consumers that the industry calls "price shoppers." This is still less than 10 percent of the overall market. Usually, price shoppers are looking for the lowest price and presume all things are equal. This is the first and usually the biggest mistake most price shoppers make.

The second, and less obvious, impact of negative media attention and influence on consumers is the pall of suspicion that has been cast over both funeral rituals and the people who provide them. Because of this, I assume that any family that doesn't know me personally has some level of suspicion about what I do or who I am. Earning their trust provides me an opportunity to educate a family on what should be valued when choosing a funeral director and funeral home. This increases the value of what we provide and the likelihood that the family will recommend our funeral home to their friends.

Funeral Directors are like any other professional or business person in that those who charge the least intend to do the least. They can't afford to do otherwise. Most funeral directors will treat a price shopper as a nuisance and will respond only to what they are directly asked. Our funeral homes welcome the price shopper because we assume they've been misinformed or poorly handled by our colleagues. We treat them as "Value Shoppers" and let them know we are not the least expensive because we provide something more than disposition services; we offer services that help those we serve begin healing.

Critics, and perhaps many of my colleagues, tend to focus on burial or cremation costs when they should focus on helping families consider how their choices will care for their emotional, relational, and spiritual needs. It would seem to me that not providing services that help families begin healing, when such resources are readily available, is the real violation of trust. What price do consumers pay for this neglect? By focusing only on price and not understanding the value of a meaningful and therapeutic ritual, those who wish to protect the vulnerable or unsuspecting inadvertently can or may cause them harm. To believe those suffering loss will receive the expert care they need without paying someone for that care aligns with the thinking of those who imagine government programs are free. Quality people and quality care *always* have a price. Sadly, the absence of both comes at a price also and this is something that industry critics often fail to acknowledge.

Divorce and the Fractured Family

Of all the psycho-social behaviors impacting the choices families make at the time of loss, perhaps none is more significant than the burden of numerous divorces within families. With 50 percent of first marriages ending in divorce and a significantly higher percentage of second marriages going the same path, the ability to determine who is responsible for or willing to make funeral arrangements can be challenging.

While the legal responsibility for this falls to the next of kin, children of divorce often want to be involved in funeral planning and this can create tension. This occurs because many children are silent as long as their parent is alive. As such, they may have concealed their distaste for their parent's second, third, or fourth spouse. When their parent dies, they are freed to express their anger and often misdirect it to the surviving spouse. The reverse is true also, with a new wife neglecting or intentionally choosing services that are against the wishes of the departed's children.

Besides the obvious hard feelings that often develop between the families in these circumstances, we may be dealing with people who could barely tolerate each other in life. In death, finding room to accommodate the needs of all is not something they are able or willing to do. This is where the word *simple* is introduced and resonates with these families. Simple cremation means simply avoiding the messiness of feeling vulnerable or confronting the injury or harm that is unresolved from earlier in life.

Sadly, families that celebrate intergenerational events are becoming a relic of the past. Families that have a biologically intact succession of great grandparents, grandparents, parents and children will soon vanish.

I must confess there are times when I'm meeting a family that I can barely stand to ask who the survivors are. This is rooted in a fear of opening a can of worms I'd rather keep shut. I'll never forget someone asking if it was okay to list in an obituary the stepchildren of a former wife of a half-brother to the ex-husband of the decedent. I guess that would make the children ex-former half-step nieces and nephews. By this standard I asked the family who in town we would leave out of the obituary! This is a light-hearted observation, but the emotional and relational wounds that are unresolved in many of these families will now remain. Death in these circumstances is a painful reminder of what was lost long before the decedent died. A meaningful therapeutic experience with loss may be the last opportunity to bring healing for the willing.

Dysfunctional Families

Drug or alcohol addiction and memories of a violent or abusive home life for many people create additional inner turmoil at the time of loss. The death of an addict or abuser is complicated for those who cared for them or were victims of their neglect or abuse. Failure to provide a time and place to begin dealing with these feelings may lead to additional emotional suppression and/or regression.

Identifying feelings of loss early on will assist the survivors of abuse by separating their feelings about the person from feelings about their death. Ritual provides the context for beginning this process. Failure to provide ritual can further complicate their grief. The blending of these emotions can be a catalyst for some to relive false feelings of personal responsibility or shame.

Ritual provides a context to separate feelings about the abuse and feelings about the death of the abuser. That ritual must be honest about the life of the decedent, not masking or rewriting the nature of their life at the time of death. Of note, I've listened several times as a victim has forgiven their perpetrator as they stood beside a lifeless body, telling them at the time of death something they could not utter in life. The fear of rejection is gone in these moments, as is the fear of being re-victimized. The words they use are sometimes of rage, occasionally regret, and often of forgiveness. They are almost always profound moments of healing. Having no ritual or choosing direct cremation or burial, will not allow for these healing possibilities.

All families have some level of dysfunction. Time in the presence of the decedent, and the survivors can provide experiences like those I have mentioned. Whether one confesses wrongs, confides affections, seeks forgiveness or offers it, these gentle moments of reflection are powerful and serve as a definitive beginning to life without the deceased. —Avoiding this process, which is almost instinctive for many, forever ends the opportunity to express these feelings. A word spoken in the presence of the dead is nearly equal to speaking it in the presence of the living. Don't underestimate the importance of this and the potential for healing for those who participate. —Conversely, a contemplative thought imagined far removed from the decedent's body will not accomplish the same.

Transient and Elitist Communities

A combination of professional development, economic opportunities, and the psycho-social issues I've mentioned previously within the United States has created an ever-growing transient population. At the core of the transient experience is a lack of attachment to the people and/or communities where the transient resides. This is a generalization that I believe is a growing phenomenon.

A hundred years ago, it was not uncommon for three generations of one family to live in the same house. Today, finding three generations of one family living in the same town is unusual. It shouldn't surprise anyone that in communities where there are three, four, or five generations of the same family, funeral rituals are common, traditional, and communal. Their attachment to the community is profound and sustained. The surest sign a family will choose ritual for themselves and others is their attachment to the deceased, their family, and the community in which they reside.

The opposite is also true. Communities where there is little social attachment and few common beliefs or sacrifices are communities where there is little shared ritual of any kind. These communities struggle to allow the heaviness of loss and feelings of vulnerability to be publicly manifested or mutually expressed. Often communities like these gather only for festive occasions. Perhaps this is why some now limit their rituals at the time of death to parties at the country club, a hall at the local university, or a nearby park.

Please understand, I don't think there is anything wrong with concluding a ritual this way, but celebrating life out of the context of the dead insures that the ritual will be an emotionally safe and relationally tidy event for all. These attributes are understandable for those who maintain superficial connections to others. Unfortunately, the emotional crash that follows these events is seldom celebrated, safe, or tidy; and is usually suffered in isolation. Ritual must account for that which is lost and that which is gained. **We celebrate what is gained as we grieve what is lost.**

Trends within the Funeral Business

I would like to offer a word of caution to both those in the business and those who are critics of it. The time for pointing the finger of exploitation is slowly coming to an end. I acknowledge that the industry as a whole has been extremely slow in learning how to help their clients in a meaningful way and that it lacked the understanding on how to best charge for their services. If current trends continue, existing market forces will cause the elimination of about 50 percent of the existing funeral homes over the next 20 years. Those in need may soon be entering a time when they will have fewer and fewer providers from which to choose. Those who applaud this as progress, or even triumph, should play the movie a little further.

Can you think of one industry where fewer providers in the market has decreased prices and increased the quality of services? Anyone with a degree in economics will tell you less competition will increase costs to consumers and decrease the quality of and type of services provided. Reducing the experience of acute loss to an economic commodity specific to only disposal costs of the dead will leave many to suffer in isolation.

Play the movie even farther and eventually funeral homes will become regional, much as hospitals are now. A local funeral in your hometown will go the way of the local hardware store. There is a reason that the national chains currently hold about a 20 percent market share of all funeral homes. Their locations are primarily in suburban communities, positioning them to maximize their "competitive potential" when smaller locations go out of business.

The average funeral home in my home state serves about 70 families a year. The vast majority of funeral homes serve small communities. They are people who know their neighbors, serve in and sacrifice for community organizations, and feel real sadness when serving those they know. Most must wait an entire career before realizing any return on their investment of time and money, and many are seeing a collapse in their business value. Most become funeral directors because they want to help others. Because of this, most enjoy high regard from their communities. This is validated by annual Gallup Polls that consistently place funeral directors among the most respected professions.

These men and women will work or are available to work 24 hours a day, 7 days a week, 365 days a year. They may serve five families in a week or five families in a month. They serve when they have colds and during times of personal or family crisis; they interrupt their family vacations, events, and activities to be ready when you need them. The picture I paint is one that is true of upwards of 80 percent of funeral directors. When you become a funeral director, you commit to a lifestyle; and you know that you will have the privilege of helping those you come to know and love during one of their greatest hours of need.

Play the movie even farther out and 20 years from now a nationally owned funeral home 30 miles from your home will dispose of your loved one. You will meet when they are available. They will have services on their schedule not yours. They will have limited or no competition, and therefore, you will pay what they charge, or you can travel another 30 miles to the next town to find out the same company owns that funeral home also. Instead of being served by someone who regularly walks with their spouse down your hometown's Main Street, you will deal with someone you don't know and who will receive the same paycheck regardless of whether you are satisfied with their service or not. If you doubt this is true, you haven't seen the direct consequence of the national firms on this industry or dealt with a Cremation Society recently.

In any industry where the primary financial transaction is reduced to a commodity, you see the emergence for a season of discount providers; this usually happens at times of consolidation. [Remember the percent of funeral homes held by national firms.] This will continue to devolve until competition leaves the market. With the entire market under the control of a couple of companies that have no local accountability, what do you think will happen to the price you pay and service you receive? Make no mistake, they will set the price you pay and you will deal with someone who punches a time clock. This kind of funeral business will have more in common with waste disposal companies. Some may think that this is alarmist. I believe some are already operating closer to this model than most are willing to admit.

The phrase "the only thing that is certain is that nothing is certain" is in play here. For now, you have choices. The choice for consumers is to choose to begin healing or postpone it. You begin healing by choosing an experience with loss that will help you and your family attend to your emotional, relational, and spiritual needs. The choice for the funeral director is status quo and (excuse the reference) slow death or to become a provider of therapeutic, interactive, and empowering experiences for the families you serve at the time of loss. The choice for critics is to expect more from those who are positioned to provide it or to continue pointing fingers that too often misdirect people from what they need. Finally, I've heard it said that we become the sum of our choices.

To all, choose wisely.

ABOUT THE AUTHOR

Karl E. Jennings

Karl is CEO of Borek Jennings Funeral Homes and the Healing Farewell Center, currently serves as President of his children's School Board and has served on numerous community boards.

He is married to his best friend, Kathleen and delighted to be father to Zachary, Joshua and Lukas. Karl is an avid golfer and enjoys date night with his wife, attending his children's activities, hosting family gatherings and swimming, fishing and snow-skiing with his family throughout their home state of Michigan.

For help planning a healing farewell
or for more information please visit:

www.healingfarewellcenter.com

PUBLISHED BY
2 MOON PRESS BOOK
PUBLISHING
800PUBLISHING.COM